ORION PLAIN AND SIMPLE

# sun signs

SASHA FENTON & JONATHAN DEE

**SEVEN DIALS**

Previously published in the United States in 2004 as *Sun Signs Made Simple* by
Sterling Publishing Company

This edition first published in Great Britain in 2019 by Seven Dials
an imprint of the Orion Publishing Group Ltd
Carmelite House, 50 Victoria Embankment
London EC4Y 0DZ

An Hachette UK Company

1 3 5 7 9 10 8 6 4 2

Interior design by Kathryn Sky-Peck

## DISCLAIMER

*The information in this book is not in any way a substitute for receiving conventional
medical treatment or consulting a physician. All the practices in this book are to be
used as an addition to existing treatments to assist the healing process and should be
fully explored only in conjunction with suitable training. Neither the author nor the
publisher assumes any liability at all for any damage caused through the application
or misapplication of procedures and statements contained in this book*

A CIP catalogue record for this book is available
from the British Library.

ISBN (Mass market paperback): 978 1 4091 7039 6
ISBN (eBook): 978 1 4091 7040 2

Printed and bound in Great Britain by Clays Ltd, Elcograf S.p.A.

www.orionbooks.co.uk

# CONTENTS

# The Bite-Sized Basics

Whether you only want to understand your own sun sign or dazzle your friends by appearing to know so much about them, our book will give you the answer because it is chock full of bite-sized astrological insights. While we hope that you find our book fun to read, the information in it works because it is based on sound astrological insights.

You can discover where a typical Gemini would love to live, the trees and plants associated with Taurus or the countries ruled by Leo. You can check out why Aquarians are hard to fathom or whether Virgos and Capricorns really *are* careful with their money.

Each chapter focuses on all mundane aspects of each sign—from health, to career, to strengths and weakness, likes and dislikes, to friends and foes, to a complete list of partner pairings by sign.

You can gain valuable insight before jumping into a love affair with a fascinating Scorpio, or discover whether your Libra friend will give you the domestic harmony you crave. If you don't crave domestic harmony, how about considering an adventurous Sagittarian or a sexy Aries?

Naturally, you will want to check out your own sun sign, but you won't be able to restrain yourself from checking out the likes, dislikes, behavior (and some of the less attractive habits) of your friends and loved ones.

There are always variations between people of the same sun sign; you are never like anyone else with your same sign. This little plain and simple book just looks at the basic traits of each sign, so if you are interested in learning more about the differences

| | | | |
|---|---|---|---|
| ♈ | Aries | Ram | March 21—April 19 |
| ♉ | Taurus | Bull | April 20—May 20 |
| ♊ | Gemini | Twins | May 21—June 21 |
| ♋ | Cancer | Crab | June 22—July 22 |
| ♌ | Leo | Lion | July 23—August 22 |
| ♍ | Virgo | Virgin | August 23—September 22 |
| ♎ | Libra | Scales | September 23—October 23 |
| ♏ | Scorpio | Scorpion | October 24—November 21 |
| ♐ | Sagittarius | Archer | November 22—December 21 |
| ♑ | Capricorn | Goat | December 22—January 19 |
| ♒ | Aquarius | Water Bearer | January 20—February 18 |
| ♓ | Pisces | Fishes | February 19—March 20 |

person to person of the same sign, my book *Unlock the Zodiac* (2019) provides a simple and effective method for understanding the subtle differences. *Unlock the Zodiac* demonstrates the variation between people born in different parts of each sign (i.e. early, middle or late in the sign). Once you have established your Decan via this easy system, you can see why you differ from others who share your sun sign.

Later in this book, you will find charts that show those people with whom you are most compatible for love, friendship and work, along with the signs with which you are unlikely to harmonize. Once again, you can check these, not only for your sun sign, but also for your Decan sign, thus producing more accuracy.

Finally, our book even shows you the best times of the year for good luck, zest, and well-being for each sun sign, as well as those times when it would be best to keep your head down . . .

# Everything
# Aries

## *(March 21–April 19)*

## Your Element—Fire

Fire signs are called the initiators of the zodiac because you don't allow the grass to grow under your feet. If a job needs to be done, there is nobody who can do it more quickly and efficiently than you, but if the job is a long-winded one that requires persistence, you may have to find someone else to come in and finish it for you. You grasp opportunities when they are offered and you don't understand those who don't have the courage and initiative to do the same themselves. Your intelligence and courage are to be admired but you can become arrogant and overbearing to those who you consider less able than you are. You can be a spendthrift, but you are as likely to spend money on others as on yourself.

## Your Quality—Cardinal

There is a kind of self-centeredness about all cardinal sign people, which means that it is hard to push you into doing things that you don't wish to do. You can come up with some great ideas but you may not always be able to carry them through to their logical conclusion. You take responsibility easily and you can care for those who are weaker than yourself, but if others try to hold you back, you will resist.

## Your Ruling Planet—Mars

Mars was once the Roman god of War and naturally this planet has always been seen as aggressive and dynamic. The ancient

Greek version is Ares (or Aries), so this planet and its sign really do fit well together. The actual planet that you can see in the sky has a slightly reddish color and it was probably the association between the color red and its association with action and activity that suggested the connection between the planet and the warlike god.

## Your Symbol—the Ram

The Ram first appeared in ancient Egypt representing the first of the gods, Ammon. This is very apt for the first sign of the zodiac. In ancient times, the sign of Aries was also symbolized by the goose, although the origins of that connection have been lost over the centuries.

## Your Appearance

There are two kinds of typical Aries look. One is tall with well-defined eyebrows—the look of the ram. The other type is small to medium in height and inclined to run to fat with chubby cheeks; you can look more like a sheep than a ram as you get older. Many of you have a reddish tinge to your hair, rather flat cheekbones and a small neat nose. Both types have a fairly wide face with a good deal of space between the ends of the eyes and brows and the side of the hairline. Many of you have a mole, scar, or some other mark on your face.

## Your Part of the Body

Aries rules the head, eyes, skull, and upper jaw.

## Your Potential Health Problems

The eyes: including conjunctivitis and squints. The head: including the upper jaw. You can suffer from headaches, sudden infections, accidents and burns, also reproductive or urinary problems. This sign also rules acts of violence.

## Your Strengths and Weaknesses

### Your Good Bits

Your best qualities are energy and initiative, a capacity for hard work and a love of life.

### Your Bad Bits

Your worst qualities are selfishness, impatience, aggression and a dislike of thoroughness.

### Your Weaknesses

You love fast vehicles and lots of partners. You can be a sucker for fast food, alcohol, creamy dishes.

## Your Favorable Locales

### Cities

Birmingham (UK), Boston (USA), Calgary, Denver, Florence, Minneapolis, Naples (Italy), Sydney (Australia).

### Countries

England, Germany, Indonesia, Japan.

## Vacations

Anywhere lively where you can sit outside and see the world go by and also spend plenty of time shopping for interesting clothes and things for your home. Some Arians are sun lovers but others find the heat uncomfortable, especially those of you who have a fair or reddish complexion.

## Landscapes

You like cities but also country areas that can offer plenty of variety.

## Your Foods

You are not a particularly fussy eater but you prefer traditional cooking or spicy or tasty food for a change. You must ensure that you don't eat too much junk food or quick food though, because it will affect your health.

## Your Style

You love anything that is new. Your taste may be plain or flamboyant but you love new things. You may need to choose designs that disguise a prominent behind.

## Your Careers

You like to work in a large organization, preferably as some kind of team leader. You are attracted to teaching, sports, medicine, and engineering. You are happy to work in a social or lifesaving organization such as the police, the armed forces and the paramilitary or as a paramedic. Once you have retired, you may take up voluntary work; this is because you like to help others and you can't sit about doing nothing. Oddly enough, many Arians are quite psychic and there are many Arian mediums and clairvoyants.

## Your Friends and Foes

- You like honest, energetic, intelligent and generous people.
- You dislike devious or indecisive types or penny-pinching nitpickers.

## Love and Sex

You prefer to be in a settled relationship, but despite this, many of you do spend some years living alone, usually after a divorce. Eventually, you find someone new and hopefully take a more balanced, less selfish view about partnerships. It is hard for any Arian to do without sex, so whether in a settled relationship or whether you are still looking around, you find ways of experiencing passion and of experimenting with your partner of the moment. Your greatest and deepest love may be for one of your children (rarely for all of them) or possibly for a pet or some other animal.

### Success in Love and Compatibility

#### Aries with Aries

You are both highly sexed, but you both like to take the lead and also lose your temper if things don't go your way, so a sense of humor will be needed.

## Aries with Taurus

Apart from certain exceptional cases, you are too different for real long-term happiness; however, a short-lived relationship might be fun.

## Aries with Gemini

This is often a successful combination unless you are selfish and the Gemini is a worrier or a grouch.

## Aries with Cancer

You are both interested in family life but you may both want to make the major decisions, so arguments are likely. Cancer likes to save money, so this could be a source of friction.

## Aries with Leo

You both like to call the shots and you both like to be the boss, so while the sexual high jinks could make this a very exciting affair, the relationship is unlikely to last.

## Aries with Virgo

You have so little in common that, unless there are other factors on your horoscopes that make for compatibility, this is hardly worth the bother.

## Aries with Libra

This combination often works because Libra likes to follow as long as he or she can respect and believe in you.

### Aries with Scorpio

This may make for a very hot and volatile affair but it is unlikely to work over the long term. At the very least, your fights would keep the neighbors from getting bored.

### Aries with Sagittarius

This is likely to be successful, especially where there are shared interests. Your sex life will be extremely interesting as well.

### Aries with Capricorn

Capricorn has a stabilizing influence on you and as long as you have shared interests, this could work, but if the Capricorn partner is prone to depression, you will soon fall out.

### Aries with Aquarius

This can be successful, because Aquarius ignores your tantrums and gets on with whatever Aquarius was doing before your explosion.

### Aries with Pisces

You may share interests in art, music or psychic matters, but your tendency to dominate would irritate Pisces, which would lead to the more sensitive Pisces to drift away from you.

# Your Possessions

## Money Attitudes

You love the stuff, as long as you have plenty of it to spend just how you want.

## The Gifts You Most Appreciate

Arians love gadgets so a pocket computer game, an electronic desk game or a new sports car would suit both males and females of the species. Both sexes also love new clothes, so a trip to the shops would be very acceptable indeed. Some love to buy sports equipment, tools, camping equipment, interesting jewelry, and unusual ornaments.

## Your Favorite Automobile

You love to drive fast and you prefer a fully automatic vehicle that doesn't involve you in much gear changing. Your favorite auto would be a company vehicle that is provided for you, looked after and paid for by someone else! If you cannot manage that, then a secondhand auto would do, especially if it is slightly unusual in some way.

## Your Ideal Home

You need plenty of space for all your junk, so a large house that includes a good attic, basement and a shed at the end of the garden would be nice. You appreciate having a room where you can keep your hobbies and knick knacks lying around.

# Entertainments

## *Your Preferred Drink*

Some Arians are prodigious drinkers; most seem to go in for beer and whisky, although you would probably drink anything that's available. Most Arians are very modest drinkers, preferring a drop of wine with a meal or an occasional spirit drink or cocktail. The odd thing is that many of you have some association with heavy drinking, either because you drink a lot or because others around you are verging on alcoholism.

## *Your Favorite Meal Out*

You love eating out and will eat almost any type of food, especially if it is interesting and well presented. However, you probably enjoy eating with your friends and family at home even more than going out to restaurants.

## *Your Night Out*

You love to sing, dance, eat, drink and be merry among friends. You love nothing better than to talk and to have a good laugh.

# Your Preferred Activities

You enjoy sports, partying, and making love.

## *Television Preferences*

None of them. You would rather do anything than sit and watch television. You like sports though, so that is probably what you watch most.

## The Books You Enjoy

You like to read biographies, history, adventure, thrillers and steamy erotic stories. Male Arians love leafing through newspapers and publications that offer items to buy or to exchange. Female Arians love clothing and household catalogues.

## The Music You Enjoy

You love music that has some kind of depth to it and this can be either classical or rock music. You enjoy old songs and folk music that you can sing along with. Many Arians have excellent singing voices.

## The Games and Sports That You Enjoy

You love energetic team games such as cricket, football, baseball or hockey along with mental games such as chess, cards, or checkers.

# Money and Luck

## Your Lucky Number

One.

## Your Money Luck

You can have the occasional windfall but most of your money luck comes as a result of working in a large organization or working for yourself and sticking to the job until your pension comes through.

## Your Correspondences

| Best Day | In ancient times, Tuesday was ascribed to the Roman god, Mars. |
|---|---|
| Worst Day | In theory, Friday is your worst day because it is associated with a planet that is traditionally different from Mars—this being Venus. However, you usually love "thank God it's Friday," because the weekend comes hard on its heels. |
| Colors | The Aries color is bright crimson red. |
| Herbs | Basil and witch hazel. |
| Tissue Salts | Calcium Phosphate. Potassium Phosphate. |
| Aromatherapy Essence | Peppermint. |
| Bach Flower Remedy | Vervain. |
| Trees | Thorn and chestnut. |
| Flowers | Honeysuckle. |
| Animals | Vulture, fox, ostrich, leopard, and of course, the sheep or ram. |
| Metal | The metal associated with your sign is iron. Iron has a low melting point and it was the metal from which weapons were made. Oxidized (rusty) iron is a reddish color. |
| Gems | Aries has various gems associated with it, especially the hard unyielding diamond and the passionate bloodstone. |

## Your Karmic Lesson

Learn to look after yourself and others; don't rely on others too much, and try to be generous, loving, and sexy.

# Everything Taurus

## (April 20–May 20)

2

## Your Element—Earth

You are practical, diligent, hard working and often happiest when doing something useful. You can be relied upon even though it might take you a while to get around to things. You are thorough and capable, but you cannot stand being harassed or rushed. You have a creative streak and your sensuality means that you know how to make things (and people) look and feel good.

Being shrewd and cautious, you need material and emotional security and you will put up with a lot in order to get it and then to keep hold of it. You may appear stingy to outsiders but this is because you fear future poverty. You cling to your family, but, being sociable, you don't usually keep outsiders at a distance.

## Your Quality—Fixed

Your fixed nature means that it takes you a while before you find the right partner, the right job or the right place to live, but once you have done so you stick to your choices as hard as you can. Sometimes you hang on too long when it would be better to let things go and this can bring you pain in the long run. You are thorough and you can finish all that you start.

## Your Ruling Planet—Venus

Venus is associated with luxury and such activities as eating, drinking and merrymaking. This is also the planet of love and sensuality.

## Your Symbol—the Bull

Myths and legends about this animal go back a long way. It was in the shape of a bull that Jupiter kidnapped Europa and founded the Cretan culture. The Cretans forever afterward worshiped the bull, calling it the earth-shaker. The bull is a symbol of strength, endurance and sexuality.

## Your Appearance

Taureans come in two shapes, but neither is tall. If you are the slim type, you might never put on weight but if you are the heavy type, you may have to watch your diet and your weight. You usually have lovely hair and eyes and a clear and glowing skin.

## Your Part of the Body

Taurus rules the lower jaw, the throat—including the thyroid gland, the neck and upper spine.

## Your Potential Health Problems

The lower jaw, lower teeth, and throat (including the thyroid gland). The neck and lower spine are delicate. Prone to weight gain.

## Your Strengths and Weaknesses

### Your Good Bits

You are thorough in all that you do, careful with money and very patient. You can put up with a lot and you don't leave anything half done. You are often brighter than you look! Many Taureans are very sociable and you make wonderful hosts and hostesses. Some of you are fabulous cooks.

## Your Bad Bits

You have a reputation for obstinacy and possessiveness. You can be very materialistic and greedy for money, possessions and food. You can have a rather nasty sarcastic and sneering manner that you use to cover feelings of inadequacy and you can be irritable when you are hungry. You may have a rather silly sense of humor.

## Your Weakness

Money, food, and possessions. Cakes and sweets.

## Your Favorable Locales

### Cities

Dublin, Hastings, Leipzig, Lucerne, Memphis, Ottawa, Parma, St. Louis, Salt Lake City.

### Countries

Iran, Ireland, Sweden, Switzerland, Turkey.

### Vacations

Anywhere that is attractive and restful. A Rhine boat trip or a visit to the tulip fields in Holland would be ideal.

### Landscapes

You enjoy country areas that have plenty of greenery, but many of you also love being on or by the sea.

## Your Foods

You love to cook and also to eat, but you are quite particular about what you put into your stomach and you like everything to be fresh and of good quality. You enjoy nice wine too. Apples, peaches and sweet flavors are traditional for your sign.

## Your Style

Conservative, comfortable and non-flashy.

## Your Careers

You love to work with your hands and also to build or create something that looks good or that has some use, so heavy activities could include farming, gardening and building. Attractive ones may include make-up artist, beautician, hairdresser, chef, fashion designer and photographer. You are interested in finance, so accountancy and banking might appeal to you. In addition to your artistic interests, you may sing, dance and act.

## Your Friends and Foes

- You like anyone who has time to sit and chat and who doesn't put you down. You don't care for those who do not appreciate the efforts that you make.
- You dislike know-it-alls who talk a lot and achieve nothing.

## Love and Sex

You are not one for moving from one partner to the next, and you are a true family person. Even if you divorce, you will try to look after your ex-partner from a distance. You rarely lose touch with

your parents or children either. Sexually, you are sensual and giv-
ing, but you don't like partners who demand unusual practices.

## Success in Love and Compatibility

### Taurus with Aries

This can work, especially if you have interests in common. You
would enjoy traveling and home-making together.

### Taurus with Taurus

You either have an instinctive mutual understanding or you
become rivals and fall out after a while.

### Taurus with Gemini

Taurus will be a stable and reassuring influence on Gemini, while
Gemini will make Taurus laugh and have fun.

### Taurus with Cancer

This is a good combination with a similar outlook and attitude to
family life, home life and finances. You may find Cancer a little
inclined to cling or to lean on you at times.

### Taurus with Leo

You are both rather obstinate, but you can care very deeply for
each other. You also both share a fondness for children or animals.

### Taurus with Virgo

This should be a success as you have much in common. What
Virgo lacks in domestic skills you supply, and what you lack in
attention to detail, Virgo supplies.

## Taurus with Libra

Your shared interests and laid-back attitude to life make you compatible. You may share similar careers and a similar attitude to domestic responsibilities and finances. This is a good combination.

## Taurus with Scorpio

This can be very successful due to the fact that you can both commit to a long-term relationship. However, it could be an absolute disaster owing to the fact that both of you are stubborn and inflexible. You may feel that Scorpio wants to hog the limelight.

## Taurus with Sagittarius

The only thing you have in common is a fondness for travel, so a true love relationship is unlikely.

## Taurus with Capricorn

This is an excellent combination, as you both enjoy home-making, gardening and doing things as a family. Neither of you enjoy the company of loud, embarrassing or messy people, so you can be safe, peaceful and comfortable.

## Taurus with Aquarius

This can be a tense relationship. You have little in common, your thinking processes are different and you are both stubborn.

## Taurus with Pisces

You both appreciate art, music, homemaking and family life and you are both sensuous so this is a good combination.

## Your Possessions

### *Money Attitudes*

You consider that money is made flat to pile up. The more you can invest in your land and property and save for a rainy day the better—until you are seduced by the selection of plants in the garden center, that is.

### *The Gifts You Most Appreciate*

Taureans of both sexes appreciate beautiful things so anything that is attractive that adds a touch of luxury will be most appreciated. You also love music, so tickets to a musical event as well as a couple of CDs go down well. A few bottles of good quality wine or a hamper of exotic food may also be a good gift idea. Ladies appreciate cosmetics, jewelry, comfy furniture and a nice night out. Both sexes love cell phones!

### *Your Favorite Automobile*

Anything that is large, comfortable and reliable.

### *Your Ideal Home*

You would prefer a large house with plenty of land around it. The house would ideally be filled with beautiful and collectable items and it should have a large kitchen and a nice dining room for entertaining your many friends.

# Entertainments

## Your Preferred Drink

Good quality wine or wine-based drinks such as sherry, port or brandy. Taureans are not usually great drinkers, so it is not often that you overdo things and get drunk.

## Your Favorite Meal Out

Quality food in a good restaurant. You like a fairly traditional meal, such as steak or lamb chops, and a good dessert is a must.

## Your Night Out

You enjoy a night at the theatre, especially if music is involved. An evening with friends or a formal occasion that requires dressing up. You also enjoy a stroll along the beach or in the countryside and a drink at an interesting country pub.

# Your Preferred Activities

You enjoy cooking, gardening and watching television.

## Television Preferences

You will watch programs about money or lifestyle programs such as gardening, doing up a home, dancing, and the arts. Otherwise, anything that you can fall asleep in front of!

## The Books You Enjoy

Useful books on gardening, cooking, homemaking. Also behind the scenes stuff, such as autobiographies, history from an insider's view, and investigative matters.

### The Music You Enjoy

Melodic classical music, opera and good pop music, especially anything you can sing along to. Taurus rules the voice so you could be an excellent singer.

### The Games and Sports that You Enjoy

You don't really like games or sports; for exercise, you enjoy dancing, and gardening.

## Money and Luck

### Your Lucky Number

Two.

### Your Money Luck

You can make money from buying, decorating and selling property and also from land, farming, building or as a result of a creative enterprise. Some Taureans gain money by inheriting it.

## Your Karmic Lesson

You need to take care of yourself and others and to ensure that you and everyone around you feel comfortable.

## Your Correspondences

| | |
|---|---|
| Best Day | This is traditionally Venus's day. |
| Worst Day | Tuesday: because this is ascribed to Mars. |
| Colors | Green and pink. |
| Herbs | Sorrel. |
| Tissue Salts | Sodium Sulphate. Sodium Phosphate. |
| Aromatherapy Essence | Sandalwood. |
| Bach Flower Remedy | Walnut. |
| Trees | Sycamore and apple. |
| Flowers | Rose, poppy, violet, foxglove, vine and clover. |
| Animals | Panther, nightingale, small farm animals and of course, the bull. |
| Metal | Copper. The colors of Taurus are pink and green, and copper is a pinkish metal that "rusts" or oxidizes to green. Copper is made from malachite, a beautiful, deep, rich green stone. Polished copper has always been used for home decoration and personal ornamentation. Copper bracelets are supposed to keep rheumatism away, so these can be helpful as you get older. |
| Gems | There are various gems associated with your sign. The deep green emerald is an obvious association for your sign but you may prefer the topaz or the sapphire. |

# Everything Gemini

*(May 21–June 21)*

3

## Your Element—Air

Yours is the element of communication, so you will always choose a job and a lifestyle that keeps you in touch with others and probably also one that takes you from one place to another. You need a variety of interests in your life and plenty of places to go and people to see. You may spend more on the phone than is healthy for your bank balance but it keeps you sane, so what the heck! Your mind is quick and you can often see solutions to other people's problems, although you are less able to solve your own problems when they arise.

## Your Quality—Mutable

You are able to adapt fairly easily to new circumstances and you appreciate a change of scenery from time to time. You don't have a very strong personality, so you are happiest when living and working with people who nurture you and who make you feel good about yourself. You love your family but you need to get away and spend a little time alone on occasion in order to recharge your emotional batteries.

## Your Ruling Planet—Mercury

The Roman god Mercury was the swift-witted messenger of the gods. His principal job was to do Jupiter's dirty work and to run errands.

## Your Symbol—the Twins

In this case, the heavenly twins, Castor and Pollux. The symbol of the heavenly twins is known in many cultures, including the Native Americans. The Bible emphasizes the rivalry of twins in the story of Cain and Abel.

## Your Appearance

While there are some overweight Geminis, most of you are small and slim. You have bright eyes and a ready smile. Your fine hair may be the bane of your life because it can be fine and difficult to control.

## Your Part of the Body

Gemini rules the upper respiratory system, the shoulders, arms, wrists, and hands.

## Your Potential Health Problems

Your weak points are your hands, arms, shoulders, upper respiratory tract and the nervous system. Gemini also rules the nervous system and the mind so any kind of nervous ailment can be expected.

## Your Strengths and Weaknesses

### Your Good Bits

You have mental agility, adaptability, the ability to communicate, and a witty sense of humor.

## Your Bad Bits

Lack of sympathy when others are ill or unhappy but you can all too easily become melancholy and self-absorbed. You may hop from one idea to another. Some Geminis don't know how to tell the truth.

## Your Weaknesses

You can spend hours chatting on the phone. Those Geminis who don't smoke make a great fuss about other people's cigarette smoke, because, inevitably, it drifts across the room toward them.

Some of you go in for alcohol, fast food and pizza, but others have a total lack of interest in food.

## Your Favorable Locales

### Cities

Bruges, Kansas City, London, Melbourne, Richmond (USA), San Francisco, Winnipeg.

### Countries

Indonesia, Japan, Wales.

### Vacations

You enjoy a good old-fashioned beach holiday where you can soak up the sun. You enjoy any place that has a variety of shops and interesting places to eat out in and also plenty to see.

## Landscapes

You like cities and interesting old towns in hilly areas.

## Your Foods

We are tempted to say, a glass of wine, a cup of coffee, a cigarette and a few vitamin pills, because many Geminis are not really into eating. When you do eat, you prefer something light and tasty. Tradition ascribes beans to your sign but oddly enough, some Geminis hate them.

## Your Style

Anything that allows you to move around quickly and which is in the latest fashion. High fashion sports clothes are ideal. You love clothes and will spend a lot of money on good ones but the real expense comes from your love of accessories.

## Your Careers

You can work in any field that involves communication, which may include being a writer, journalist, teacher, telephone operator and sales-person. Travel is also an important part of many Gemini careers, so you could become a taxi-driver, courier, travel agent, cabin-crew, or pilot of an airplane.

## Your Friends and Foes

- Your friends must be intelligent, humorous people who have interesting lives.
- You hate dull, mean or crabby types, and you have little patience for quiet or introverted people or spiteful and offensive ones.

## Love and Sex

You tend to fall in love deeply, but tend to choose selfish or unloving partners. If you can see where you are going wrong after one or two mistakes you will be fine; otherwise you will find yourself acting as a servient, emotional, or physical punching-bag to one partner after another. You are experimental where sex is concerned because you can get bored by the same old routine.

### Success in Love and Compatibility

#### Gemini with Aries

This can be a good combination unless Aries is too bossy or selfish. You can think up ideas for Aries to carry out.

#### Gemini with Taurus

You are so different that it is either a case of opposites attracting each other, or there is nothing to hold this relationship together.

#### Gemini with Gemini

You may understand each other completely and create an atmosphere of total harmony, or you can get each other down by both demanding attention at the same time.

## Gemini with Cancer

You probably share enough similarities and interests to keep you happy. Cancer will mother you and this could be just what you most need.

## Gemini with Leo

This can work well because you share a great sense of humor, but you can both become extremely downhearted at times so you must guard against depressing each other.

## Gemini with Virgo

You share interests and you may have plenty of patience for each other's worries and neuroses. Virgo's stubborn behavior may aggravate you at times.

## Gemini with Libra

This should be an easy relationship as long as you don't expect the world from your Libran partner. You should have a similar sex drive, so that helps things along.

## Gemini with Scorpio

This is a poor combination as Scorpio will dominate you and you will use sarcasm in return. It could work for a short-term fling but that is about all.

## Gemini with Sagittarius

Your Sagittarian partner will make you laugh and you share many interests, so this should be a good one for the long haul. Your partner needs plenty of freedom, so avoid clinging too tightly.

### Gemini with Capricorn

A similar outlook on family life can make this work, although this is not the easiest of combinations, as Capricorn may seek to dominate you.

### Gemini with Aquarius

This is an excellent combination as long as Aquarius is not too detached. You will make your Aquarian partner laugh and you will certainly have plenty to chat about.

### Gemini with Pisces

This can work as you are both adaptable, but Pisces may irritate you and you may also want more commitment than Pisces can handle.

## Your Possessions

### Money Attitudes

Your Symbol of the twins makes you a complex and double-sided personality and nowhere does this show more than in the way you approach financial matters. You usually ensure that you can pay your bills, but you can go nuts when you are let loose in a shop that sells clothing and accessories.

### The Gifts You Most Appreciate

Stationery of any kind appeals to you and a good quality pen and pencil set or a math set would suit some of you. Airline tickets to a hot place would delight you, as would a hands-on day at a racetrack. You love books, computer equipment, cell phones and electronic address books. Additionally, anything in a clever box or bag, such as make-up, bathroom stuff, and a manicure set.

## Your Favorite Automobile

A small, fast sports vehicle suits you best. Even if you have absolutely no money at all, you need to be mobile and, therefore, you will put up with any kind of broken down transport rather than to be without wheels.

## Your Ideal Home

A home in an area where the air is fresh and there is room for a garden. Plenty of storage space for your vast collection of gadgets and at least three telephones! You also need a maid to do the cleaning and ironing for you and someone to clean up the mess that your animals leave.

# Entertainments

## Your Preferred Drink

This is quite an addictive sign and a great many Geminis drink quite heavily. Even light drinkers enjoy spirits, wine, beer or lager with a meal. Cocktails and mixed drinks are liked too.

## Your Favorite Meal Out

Question: what does the Gemini make for dinner? Answer: reservations! You prefer simple foods like fish and chips or salads to over-cooked dishes or piles of unidentified mush. Many Geminis enjoy Chinese food, because it consists of tasty titbits. Many of you are vegetarians. Most of you are happy with a drink, a cigarette, and the occasional tomato sandwich to keep you from keeling over.

## Your Night Out

You love to dress up in nice clothes, so you like to go to places where you can show these off. You don't like crowds, so a classy restaurant where you can sit with a few friends or a quiet cocktail bar is great. You also enjoy music so anything from a pop show to a visit to the opera suits you.

## Your Preferred Activities

Shopping, talking with friends, spending time with your children and pets.

## Television Preferences

You probably spend more time reading than watching television but when you do watch, you either choose something intelligent, such as a documentary or an escapist film with a clever plot and a good script.

## The Books You Enjoy

You like to read about people but you also enjoy reading magazines, newspapers, and psychology and astrology books.

### The Music You Enjoy

You like anything with clever or meaningful lyrics and compilations.

### The Games and Sports That You Enjoy

Your sports are badminton, tennis, word games, and board games.

## Money and Luck

### Your Lucky Number

Three.

### Your Money Luck

A surprising number of Geminis gain money by marrying a wealthy partner. If this doesn't happen, then you are most likely to work for your wealth.

## Your Correspondences

| Best Day | Wednesday: because it is associated with the Roman god, Mercury. |
| --- | --- |
| Worst Day | Friday. |
| Colors | Astrological tradition suggests yellow, black and white check and multicolored mixtures. |
| Herbs | Marjoram. |
| Tissue Salts | Calcium Sulphate. Ferrous Phosphate. Potassium Chloride. |
| Aromatherapy Essence | Eucalyptus. |
| Bach Flower Remedy | Larch. |
| Trees | Nut trees, especially the walnut. |
| Flowers | Tradition suggests that your plants are the lily of the valley, lavender, orchid, and the gladiolus. |
| Animals | Hyena, monkey, parrot, and stork. |
| Metal | Mercury. |
| Gems | There are various gems associated with your sign, including the agate, alexandrite, and onyx. |

## Your Karmic Lesson

Your job in this lifetime is to be a friend and to communicate with others. You may also need to do something to help those who are worse off than yourself.

# Everything Cancer

*(June 22–July 22)*

4

### Your Element—Water

This is the element of emotion and you are certainly sensitive and emotional. Your feelings run deep but you can also allow your emotions to spill over into areas of your life where logic would serve you better. You can make decisions on the spur of the moment that are based on your feelings at the time, and this can lead you to regret those decisions later in life.

### Your Quality—Cardinal

There is a kind of self-centeredness about all cardinal sign people, which means that it is hard to push you into doing things that you don't wish to do. You can come up with some great ideas but you may not always be able to carry them through. You take responsibility easily and you care for those who are weaker than yourself. If others try to hold you back, you will resist.

### Your Ruling Planet—the Moon

The Moon represents the feminine principal and it is connected to the idea of travel and the sea. The Moon is associated with many classical goddesses including Persephone, and Selene, also known as Luna. This sign also relates to Artemis or Diana, the virgin huntress who was the twin sister of Apollo.

### Your Symbol—the Crab

The crab has a hard shell and a soft and tasty interior, just like you. It also goes about things in a sideways direction, which you also do on occasion. Legend says that the crab was thrown into the sky for pinching Hercules on the toe while he was involved in one of his difficult labors.

## Your Appearance

You are usually of middle height or even a little on the tall side. Some of you gain weight later in life, especially around the top half of your body. Your hair is abundant and healthy and you have slightly rounded cheeks and a nice smile.

## Your Part of the Body

The lungs, breast and rib cage; the stomach and digestive organs.

## Your Potential Health Problems

Your weak spots are the chest, thorax, lower lungs and breasts and also the stomach and upper digestive system. Poor eating habits may cause trouble. You may retain body fluids.

## Your Strengths and Weaknesses

### Your Good Bits

You are a good listener and a kind-hearted and sympathetic friend. Your family relies on you and friends can always count on you.

### Your Bad Bits

You can be moody and bad tempered without being able to explain what has made you feel like that. You can cling to your family.

### Your Weaknesses

You worry about everything—especially money—and you can be a misery at times.

You can overindulge on chocolate, sweet desserts, bread and things to spread on it. You may not bother with alcohol, but you may like the occasional glass of medium-sweet wine.

## Your Favorable Locales

### Cities

Atlanta, Amsterdam, Christchurch, Manchester, New York, Vancouver, Venice.

### Countries

Holland, Mauritius, New Zealand, Scotland, the USA (which is itself Cancerian, because it was born on the fourth of July).

### Vacations

You love being close to or on water, especially the sea. You are nervous of strange foods, so you tend to visit traditional places that don't spring dietary surprises on you.

### Landscapes

Green areas near water and places that offer sea views.

## Your Foods

Cancerians love to eat and you prefer a properly cooked meal; your stomach is delicate, so you may prefer not to eat highly spiced dishes. Chocolate and other sweet things appeal to you, as does a traditional Christmas dinner. You are not much of a drinker but you appreciate a little fine wine on occasion.

## Your Style

You favor rather formal clothes in attractive colors such as lavender or pale greens and blues. Once you are out of your teens and early twenties, you avoid funky or strange garments.

## Your Careers

You like small-scale business, so owning your own shop may appeal. Also antique dealer, teacher, nurse, chef, hotelier, manager and anything related to teaching and caring for small children or older people.

## Your Friends and Foes

- You like gentle, home-loving types and also business people who talk your language. You prefer people who understand your need for privacy.
- You dislike rude, brash, noisy, intrusive and unhelpful people.

## Love and Sex

You love every member of your family, even if they get on your nerves! You can even take on step- or grandchildren and bring them up as your own. In love, you are passionate and caring but you can also be surprisingly demanding. Some of you show your love by cooking for your partner, while others enjoy pleasing a partner in bed. You are not notably adventurous in bed. Love and affection count for more with you than sexual fireworks.

## Success in Love and Compatibility

### Cancer with Aries

You share a love of home life and concern for the family so this can be a good match. Aries will try to dominate, but you won't allow your partner to get away with too much of that kind of behavior.

### Cancer with Taurus

You have lots in common and a similar attitude to love, sex, family life and money, so this looks very good indeed. You will have some wonderful vacations together.

### Cancer with Gemini

You mother Gemini, and Gemini likes being mothered. In return, Gemini will make you laugh, give you plenty of attention and get you out of the house from time to time.

### Cancer with Cancer

This combination is either extremely harmonious, or else you are too alike to keep each other interested for very long.

### Cancer with Leo

This should not work at all, but oddly, it does. You both love family life and you both need the stability that the other can offer.

### Cancer with Virgo

You are both caring and somewhat self-sacrificial so you should get along quite easily. However, Virgo is quiet and logical, so your partner may find your emotionalism hard to cope with.

## Cancer with Libra

You like to be in charge and to make decisions and Libra is indecisive, so this could work well. You will either be content together or argue fiercely.

## Cancer with Scorpio

You are both intuitive and apt to make decisions based on the way you feel at any moment in time. As long as your emotions run in tandem, this can work—as long as Scorpio is not too domineering.

## Cancer with Sagittarius

You have so little in common that this stands very little chance of working. You like to cling while Sagittarius needs freedom and your priorities are utterly different.

## Cancer with Capricorn

This can be an excellent combination as you have much in common. You may find it easiest if you are the homemaker and Capricorn the money-earner.

## Cancer with Aquarius

You will find it extremely difficult to understand each other as your thought processes are different; this is not an easy match.

## Cancer with Pisces

You are both intuitive, sensitive, and think in similar ways; however, Pisces needs more freedom than you might wish to give.

## Your Possessions

### Money Attitudes

Most of the time you are careful to the point of stinginess, but you can splash out heavily on travel and also on your loved ones.

### The Gifts You Most Appreciate

Cancerians are supposed to be home loving, and so you are. Nevertheless, you love to get away on trips, outings and holidays, therefore tickets to an outing, a trip or any kind of event suits you nicely. You love music so tickets to a show or a pop concert would also be nice. Gadgets for the kitchen and nice tableware are also appreciated. You also love albums, silver ornaments and jewelry. Also antiques, coins, or anything else that can be collected.

### Your Favorite Automobile

This would probably be a minibus that holds the family, the dogs and all the shopping. You cannot cope with a small vehicle, as it would never be able to carry all your junk.

### Your Ideal Home

You like living with, or close to, family members in a happy atmosphere. You prefer an older building and when you find the right one you tend to stay put. You may add on an in-law apartment for visiting relatives and friends.

# Entertainments

## *Your Preferred Drink*

You are not much of a drinker so you are probably happiest with a cup of tea.

## *Your Favorite Meal Out*

You are an excellent cook and a discriminating diner. You enjoy French food, made with the freshest ingredients and cooked to perfection. You would not hesitate to ask for the recipe.

## *Your Night Out*

You enjoy going to the theatre, so any kind of show, play, musical, opera, or performance goes down well with you. Otherwise, you enjoy a trip to the cinema.

# Your Preferred Activities

Relaxing with friends and your loved ones, and also cooking for them. You love being with people who make you laugh. You also love to travel with people who make you happy.

## *Television Preferences*

Soap operas, history, nature, geography, wildlife and travel documentaries. You also may like reality TV, just for its strangeness.

## *The Books You Enjoy*

You like stories that are set in exotic locations. You also enjoy reading history, historical romance, murder mysteries, and books on travel or the armed services.

### The Music You Enjoy

You love nostalgic music that brings back pleasant memories, along with soft pop or popular classical music.

### The Games and Sports That You Enjoy

You like football, walking and exploring. You have an excellent memory so games of strategy such as Othello, Connect Four, and card games such as bridge or poker may appeal.

## Money and Luck

### Your Lucky Number

Four.

### Your Money Luck

You can inherit money or be given it by other members of your family. Otherwise, you gain money by buying and selling property.

## Your Karmic Lesson

Your karmic destiny is to take care of others and to make a nice home. Also to stretch your imagination by reading, thinking, talking and traveling to interesting places. You should try to control your moods and to avoid taking decisions that are based on the way that you feel at any moment in time.

## Your Correspondences

| | |
|---|---|
| Best Day | Monday. Traditionally this is the Moon's day. |
| Worst Day | Wednesday. |
| Colors | White, silver and all pearly or oyster shades. |
| Herbs | Rosemary and comfrey. |
| Tissue Salts | Calcium Fluoride. Silica. Sodium Phosphate. |
| Aromatherapy Essence | Coriander. |
| Bach Flower Remedy | Honeysuckle. |
| Trees | Traditionally willow, but also the mangrove, because this also grows near or in water; the Australian paper-bark tree as well, for much the same reason. |
| Flowers | Acanthus, lotus (water lily) and wild flowers. Cancerians have a good memory, therefore, rosemary for remembrance. |
| Animals | Crab, lobster, tortoise, owl, otter, cuckoo, and frog. |
| Metal | Silver. |
| Gems | The pearl and also mother of pearl. |

# Everything
# Leo
*(July 23—August 22)*

## Your Element—Fire

Fire signs are called the initiators of the zodiac, because you don't allow the grass to grow under your feet. If a job needs to be done, there is nobody who can do it more quickly and efficiently than you, but if the job is a long-winded one that requires persistence, you may have to find someone else to come in and finish it for you. You grasp opportunities when they are offered and you don't understand those who don't have the courage and initiative to do the same themselves. Your intelligence and courage are to be admired, but you can become arrogant and overbearing to those who you consider less able than you are. You can be a spendthrift, but you are as likely to spend money on others as on yourself.

## Your Quality—Fixed

Your fixed nature means that it takes you a while before you find the right partner, the right job or the right place to live, but once you have done so you stick to your choices as hard as you can. Sometimes you hang on too long when it would be better to let things go and this can bring you pain in the long run.

## Your Ruling Planet—the Sun

The Sun is associated with the Roman god, Apollo who was the god of music, poetry, prophecy, reason, light and healing.

## Your Symbol—the Lion

This commemorates the first of the labors of Hercules, which was the defeat of the Nemean lion. The lion has always been associated with strong men. Samson also fought a lion. Many Leos actually look a bit like the king of the jungle.

## Your Appearance

Typical Leos are medium or slightly less in height and usually medium in weight as well, although they may put on weight later in life. The best feature is likely to be their hair, which is abundant and slightly wavy. Both sexes like long hair when young, but females may cut their hair shorter later for the sake of convenience while men tend to get a little thin on top. Leo eyes are small and sometimes quite deep set, so female Leos usually wear a lot of eye make-up to make their eyes look larger.

## Your Part of the Body

The parts of the body associated with Leo are the spine, heart, arteries, and circulation.

## Your Potential Health Problems

Your potentially troublesome areas are the spine, the heart, the arteries, and circulation.

## Your Strengths and Weaknesses

### Your Good Bits

You are honest, decent, hard working and a good organizer. You rarely give up or give in to despair. You are extremely generous and affectionate, and you don't tell others what they should do or how they should live.

### Your Bad Bits

You can be arrogant and bad tempered when you don't get your own way or when you are fatigued or hungry. You are also self-centered and, sometimes, extravagant.

### Your Weaknesses

You enjoy being the center of attention and also being the boss. You are a sucker for smoked salmon, Chinese food, chocolate éclairs, sushi and anything that is expensive. You are not really into alcohol, but you may enjoy the occasional glass of wine, sweet liqueur or cocktail.

## Your Favorable Locales

### Cities

Blackpool, Bombay, Chicago, Damascus, Labrador City (Canada), Los Angeles, Portsmouth (UK), Prague, Philadelphia, Rome.

### Countries

Czech Republic, France, Italy, Romania, Slovakia.

## Vacations

Anywhere that is expensive, sophisticated, exotic, and luxurious. A lavish cruise would appeal to you.

## Landscapes

Wide open spaces, mountains, forests, and green valleys.

## Your Foods

Astrological tradition suggests saffron and citrus fruits because of their golden or yellow color. You are not a particularly fussy eater, as you can enjoy anything that is beautifully cooked.

## Your Style

Classy, colorful clothes—preferably with designer labels.

## Your Careers

You are not comfortable when working under others or as part of a team, so you must be in charge. Yours is the sign of the entrepreneur or manager but you can also shine in any creative or artistic field, especially if it includes performing or teaching. You can work with children or in any field that is glamorous and that carries a sense of status.

## Your Friends and Foes

- You prefer to keep company with interesting and even somewhat outrageous people who achieve success in their own field.

- You can't stand bullies, whiners or dull and pompous people, or those who try to upstage you.

## Love and Sex

You are one of the most affectionate signs of the zodiac, so you can give a great deal of love to those who you care about. You are also a good friend and a wonderful parent. You also need a lot of affection and you demand loyalty and a high standard of behavior from a partner—perhaps too high in some cases. You are extremely highly sexed but you get tired quickly so you may not be inclined to make love if you are working too hard in other areas of your life.

## *Success in Love and Compatibility*

### Leo with Aries

You are both extremely competitive and you will each struggle to be top dog, so this is not a comfortable long-term situation—but a short-term love affair would be exciting.

### Leo with Taurus

This might work in some cases but Taurus is slow and apt to be content with life without making the effort to do more or to become more, and this could irritate you.

### Leo with Gemini

This can be a nice combination as long as neither is too restless and as long as you don't both become downhearted at the same time.

## Leo with Cancer

Technically speaking, this should not work at all, as Cancer is too emotional for you, but your shared interests in family life can compensate for any occasional problems that you may experience.

## Leo with Leo

Frankly, this works better as a friendship than as a long-term love relationship, probably because you are too similar and both want to be the boss.

## Leo with Virgo

As long as Virgo is not neurotic and self-obsessed, this can work, and at least you will make each other laugh.

## Leo with Libra

There is a tremendous sexual attraction here but Libra's habit of switching off and withdrawing into a kind of dream world might put you off. There could also be a fight for supremacy.

## Leo with Scorpio

Oddly enough, this match is often very successful as you both like to make a commitment to family life, but Scorpio can go on about things sometimes, and this bores you.

## Leo with Sagittarius

This can work as long as the Sagittarian has some common sense and is prepared to commit to the long haul—otherwise it would make a fun short-term fling.

### Leo with Capricorn

As long as the Capricorn is sociable and outgoing, this works fine, but if your partner is the workaholic depressive type, you will soon get bored.

### Leo with Aquarius

You are both stubborn, but if your thinking is along similar lines, you can make a success of this one. Aquarius is less interested in children and family life than you are.

### Leo with Pisces

Both of you are creative and attracted to show biz and glamour, so you may have many shared interests, but Pisces habit of drinking or escapism will irritate you.

## Your Possessions

### Money Attitudes

You certainly know how to spend lots of money in great style, so you ensure that you also earn lots of money in great style. The biggest drain on your resources comes from your amazing generosity to your friends and loved ones.

### The Gifts You Most Appreciate

Leos love luxury and gold is their lucky metal, so gold jewelry or a gold watch would please you. You might appreciate a year's membership of an up-market health or country club. Another great gift is a holiday in the sun.

## Your Favorite Automobile

The most expensive and nicely appointed vehicle will do nicely. Better still, a sober vehicle for work and a fun one for weekends.

## Your Ideal Home

A large, luxurious home in a nice area would suit you. Your home is neither untidy nor surgically clean—it is comfortable with excellent quality goods and furnishings that you live with for as long as possible before replacing. However, your electrical and hi-fi equipment is usually brand new. There must be a garden or play area for your children and their friends.

# Entertainments

## Your Preferred Drink

Most Leos can't drink much alcohol and are teetotalers. If you do drink, it is likely to be wine, champagne, or perhaps a mixed drink with plenty of ice. Your favorite drink is probably tea or coffee.

## Your Favorite Meal Out

You enjoy the best of the best, and that includes good service, excellent presentation and clean linen. Many Leos enjoy a buffet or a salad bar.

## Your Night Out

You love to have a good laugh with your friends and the setting is less important than the company is as far as you are concerned. Otherwise, you enjoy the theater or a walk in an attractive park on a summer's night.

## Your Preferred Activities

You enjoy playing light sports, traveling, and being with your family. You also enjoy gardening and homemaking.

### Television Preferences

You are too busy living to bother much with the television, but when you do watch it must be something interesting. You have no patience for soap operas or "reality" shows where people are shut up with others for a week until they start screaming at each other.

### The Books You Enjoy

You love "a good read," so novels that have a large scope appeal to you. You enjoy adventure stories, science fiction, thrillers, murder mysteries, and the occasional romantic story.

### The Music You Enjoy

Lively music, light classical music, dance tunes, romantic pop music.

### The Games and Sports That You Enjoy

Leos are often keen on swimming but you also enjoy tennis and badminton. You love to dance and you may take lessons so that you can do this well.

## Money and Luck

### Your Lucky Number

Five.

## Your Money Luck

You work for your money. Small windfalls can come your way but in general, you gain wealth by your own efforts.

## Your Karmic Lesson

You need to get over any childhood hang-ups and shyness and push yourself into the limelight. You need to give love and to find it, but most of all you need to learn to love yourself. You also need children or pets that you can love to distraction.

## Your Correspondences

| | |
|---|---|
| Best Day | Sunday: this is the Sun's day. |
| Worst Day | Saturday. |
| Colors | Gold, yellow, creamy shades and orange. |
| Herbs | Chamomile, saffron, rosemary. |
| Tissue Salts | Magnesium Phosphate. Calcium Phosphate. |
| Aromatherapy Essence | Garlic. |
| Bach Flower Remedy | Vine. |
| Trees | Ash and palm. |
| Flowers | Marigold, nasturtium, sunflower and cyclamen. |
| Animals | Lion, starfish, crocodile, swan, peacock. |
| Metal | Gold. |
| Gems | There are various gems associated with your sign, such as the diamond, zircon, ruby, sardonyx, and tiger's eye. |

# Everything Virgo

## 6

*(August 23–September 22)*

## Your Element—Earth

You are practical, diligent, hard working, and often happiest when doing something useful. You can be relied upon, even though it might take you a while to get around to things. You are thorough and capable but you can't stand being harassed or rushed. You have a creative streak and your sensuality means that you know how to make things (and people) look and feel good. Being shrewd and cautious, you need material and emotional security and you will put up with a lot in order to get it and then to keep hold of it. You may appear stingy to outsiders but this is because you fear future poverty. You cling to your family, but being sociable, you don't usually keep outsiders at a distance.

## Your Quality—Mutable

You are able to adapt fairly easily to new circumstances and you appreciate a change of scenery from time to time. You don't have a very strong personality, so you are happiest when living and working with people who nurture you and who make you feel good about yourself. You love your family but you need to get away and spend a little time alone on occasion in order to recharge your emotional batteries.

## Your Ruling Planet—Mercury

Mercury was the messenger of the gods who also did Jupiter's dirty work for him. He was the god of travelers, healing, of magic and also of thieves.

## Your Symbol—the Virgin

This represents the mother goddess who presided over the gathering in of food. To think of Virgo as a prudish old maid is a mistake because she is only one of the aspects of the great goddess or mother figures of mythology. Perhaps this is a girl who will be a mother at some future date but might also be a particularly loving big sister. This sign is also associated with the harvest and with the storage of foodstuffs.

## Your Appearance

You may be slightly above average height and your habit of holding your head up gives you a stately manner. Your bone structure is good, so as long as you don't put on too much weight later in life, you can continue to look good well into old age.

## Your Part of the Body

Your sign rules the lower digestive system and the bowels. It also concerns the skin, nervous system, and the mind.

## Your Potential Health Problems

Your weak areas are the lower digestive system, intestines and bowels. Others are the skin, nervous system, and the mind. Funny diets could possibly affect your health badly.

## Your Strengths and Weaknesses

### Your Good Bits

You are kind hearted and hard working, and you have the patience with detail needed to cope with craftwork. You are a great conversationalist and you have a wonderful sense of humor.

### Your Bad Bits

You can be fussy, critical and a hypochondriac and you are prone to tell others how they should live.

### Your Weaknesses

You are prone to self-punishment, low self-esteem, and being far too quick to criticize yourself and others. You can be sarcastic and hurtful if you feel hurt yourself.

You can indulge in cookies and cakes, as well as chocolate when you feel depressed.

## Your Favorable Locales

### Cities

Cheltenham, Heidelberg, Jerusalem, Paris, Phoenix, Reading, Saskatoon (Canada).

### Countries

Canada, Greece, West Indies.

### Vacations

You need relaxing places where you can switch off from work and worry; however, you are easily bored, so visit interesting places.

## Landscapes

You love gardens, pretty villages, and places that have some history attached to them.

## Your Foods

Some Virgos are extremely fussy about food and many of you are vegetarians. If you are not fussy, you enjoy everything except for one or two things that you were forced to eat in childhood.

## Your Style

You dress in a neat and smart style, preferring casual or sporty clothes that don't get in your way or hold you up. Many Virgos suffer from painful feet so good shoes are a must.

## Your Careers

You love to serve others. You also have an interest in health and healing, so many of you work in the medical field or even in that of spiritual healing. Other careers might be those of nutritionist, writer, teacher, healer, secretary, skilled manual work, art, computer programmer, and astrologer.

## Your Friends and Foes

- You appreciate logical and intelligent people with a good sense of humor, who work hard for what they get in life.
- You dislike materialistic or unrealistic people; also those who are rude, overly critical, abrupt or who seek to put you down.

## Love and Sex

You show your love for others by doing things for them as opposed to showing outright affection. You are the most loyal and courageous friend in the zodiac. Sexually, you can be quite experimental and more promiscuous than most people would imagine.

### Success in Love and Compatibility

**Virgo with Aries**

Aries's impulsiveness and hot temper will upset you and you would soon feel squashed and dominated, so this is not an affair that we would recommend.

**Virgo with Taurus**

You have much in common, although you will run rings around Taurus intellectually while your partner will be more creative than you are. As long as Taurus is happy with that situation, all will be well.

**Virgo with Gemini**

You could be happy together as long as neither of you is too much of a worrier. You are very similar in many ways and you can both adapt well to new situations.

**Virgo with Cancer**

You are both caring types and you share many interests, so this is a good match. Cancer will encourage you to talk over your problems while you will stimulate your partner's intellect.

## Virgo with Leo

This works well because practicality allied to Leo's creativity can make quite a good match. You both enjoy home life and entertaining so your home could be full of laughter.

## Virgo with Virgo

As with all same-sign relationships, this is either great or competitive, particularly as you are both rather stubborn.

## Virgo with Libra

You will have a have a hard time pinning the Libran down and you may find yourself arguing about relatively unimportant matters, so this is not a comfortable match.

## Virgo with Scorpio

You both have unresolved issues from your childhoods; this will either give you things in common or put you at odds with each other. Scorpio may try to dominate, and you will dig in your heels.

## Virgo with Sagittarius

You share a great sense of humor and you both need space in your lives, so this can work quite well. However, Sagittarius may be less interested in a long-term relationship than you are.

## Virgo with Capricorn

You have a certain amount in common and are both practical, but you are less interested in looking after your parents and in-laws than a Capricorn. Additionly, a Capricorn may depress you or try to dominate you.

### Virgo with Aquarius

This is not an easy relationship, as you both have your own ways of going about things. Aquarius's vagueness may irritate you while your partner may find your chatter annoying.

### Virgo with Pisces

You tend to take on people who need to be rescued and Pisces definitely needs this, but once you have solved one of Pisces's problems, your partner will present you with another. You could become frustrated with this in the long run.

## Your Possessions

### *Money Attitudes*

Sometimes you have money and at other times you don't, but you always manage to get by somehow or other, perhaps by taking on extra work of some kind.

### *The Gifts You Most Appreciate*

You have many interests. Gifts of sports gear, books on your special interest, or gardening tools might do the trick. Many Virgos enjoy cooking, so kitchen equipment or recipe books are acceptable. You like nice clothes, bathroom items, and desk organizers.

### *Your Favorite Automobile*

Your sign is ruled by Mercury, the fleet-footed messenger of the gods and Virgo is bracketed by (and infected by) expansive Leo and irresponsible Libra. Therefore, you probably tend to choose something fast, efficient and way out of your price range.

## Your Ideal Home

You like a house with enough room for a library or office. You enjoy a garden as long as it isn't too large for you to keep up, because you would hate to see it go to seed. You might choose to live in an apartment as long as you have a nice view from the window.

## Entertainments

### Your Preferred Drink

Many Virgos are beer enthusiasts and some search out special beers that are brewed by small local breweries. Otherwise you are either not fussy as long as there is something around to drink, or you don't drink any alcohol at all.

### Your Favorite Meal Out

You may be a very fussy eater, limiting yourself to a small choice of foods. Otherwise, you will eat anything that is familiar to you.

### Your Night Out

You like the theatre and the opera, but you also enjoy a quiz evening in a pub. Some of you enjoy playing cards or chess with a group of like-minded people.

## Your Preferred Activities

Yours is not a particularly active sign in the sporting sense, so you prefer quiet pursuits such as reading, listening to music or gossiping with your many friends. Many of you enjoy cooking for your friends, because you enjoy the creative aspect of this.

### Television Preferences

You enjoy strange and clever programs that get you thinking. You also enjoy children's television, and quizz and game shows. Your sense of humor means that you love comedy programs.

### The Books You Enjoy

History, factual books and "did you know" type reference books, and philosophy and intellectual books. You also like stories of pure imagination, such as science fiction.

### The Music You Enjoy

Jazz, classical music; cool, clever music of any kind.

### The Games and Sports That You Enjoy

Chess, quizzes, scrabble, board games, and crosswords. Walking, exploring alone or with a friend. Sports as such don't interest you much, although you may possibly like games of skill such as billiards or golf.

## Money and Luck

### Your Lucky Number

Six.

### Your Money Luck

You work for your money but you can receive small windfalls from time to time. Some of you can profit by marrying money.

## Your Karmic Lesson

You are bound to spend some part of your life sacrificing your own needs for those of others.

## Your Correspondences

| Best Day | Wednesday: this is associated with the Roman god, Mercury. |
|---|---|
| Worst Day | Thursday. |
| Colors | Navy blue, muted greens, mulberry, browns, gray, and pastel shades. |
| Herbs | Parsley and dill. |
| Tissue Salts | Potassium Sulphate. Silica. Sodium Chloride. |
| Aromatherapy Essence | Orange. |
| Bach Flower Remedy | Rock water. |
| Trees | Nut trees, especially hazel. |
| Flowers | Cornflowers, small brightly colored flowers, snowdrop, lily, and narcissus. |
| Animals | Squirrel, greyhound, weasel, swallow. |
| Metal | Mercury. |
| Gems | There are various gems associated with your sign, including the Sardonyx, diamond, and the chrysolite. |

# Everything
# Libra
*(September 23—October 23)*

**7**

## Your Element—Air

Yours is the element of communication, so you will always choose a job and a lifestyle that keeps you in touch with others and probably also one that takes you from one place to another. You need a variety of interests in your life and plenty of places to go and people to see. You may spend more on the phone than is healthy for your bank balance but it keeps you sane, so what the heck! Your mind is quick and you can often see solutions to other people's problems, although you are less able to solve your own problems when they arise.

## Your Quality—Cardinal

There is a kind of self-centeredness about all cardinal sign people, which means that it is hard to push you into doing things that you don't wish to do. You can come up with some great ideas but you may not always be able to carry them through to their logical conclusion. You take responsibility easily and you can care for those who are weaker than yourself, but if others try to hold you back, you will resist.

## Your Ruling Planet—Venus

Venus was the Roman goddess of love and romance. Venus is also associated with luxury and such activities as eating, drinking, lovemaking and merrymaking.

## Your Symbol—the Scales

When writing in the first century AD, the poet Manilius said of this sign, "Day and night are weighed in Libra's scales, equal a while, at last the night prevails." This suggests the order of light and darkness. The scales obviously have something to do with weighing and measuring and also the legal profession. Librans like to weigh up all sides of an argument before making a decision.

## Your Appearance

You are one of the luckier signs of the zodiac where looks are concerned because Librans run from being merely attractive to very good looking indeed. Your pleasant smile and manner also help you to look good.

## Your Part of the Body

Your traditional body parts are the soft organs of the bladder and kidneys. Libra also rules the ability to move and walk and it can be associated with the lower spine.

## Your Potential Health Problems

Your weak areas are the soft organs such as the pancreas, bladder, and kidneys. You can also experience problems with movement due to problems with the lower spine or the neck area.

## Your Strengths and Weaknesses

### Your Good Bits

You are pleasant, charming and friendly but also fair minded and a good arbitrator.

### Your Bad Bits

You can be lazy, indecisive and totally unrealistic. You can argue the hind leg off a donkey when you feel like doing so.

### Your Weaknesses

You enjoy sex, pleasure and luxury. You can be too fond of alcohol, rich expensive foods and scrumptious desserts. If you start to drink, it can end in a real binge if you are not careful.

## Your Favorable Locales

### Cities

Antwerp, Copenhagen, Frankfurt, Indianapolis, Lisbon, Montreal, Nottingham, Sacramento, Vienna.

### Countries

Austria, Argentina, Burma, Japan, Tibet.

### Vacations

You enjoy spending your vacation in luxurious surroundings where you can be sure of good food and excellent service. If there is a chance to flirt with the locals, so much the better! You also enjoy short city breaks.

## Landscapes

Open countryside; the seaside, along with sunny, fresh and breezy places. You also like cities with all their sophisticated attractions.

## Your Foods

You love to eat out in good restaurants. At home, you prefer small, nicely presented dishes. Astrological tradition suggests that the cherry and the pomegranate resonate with your sign.

## Your Style

You love looking good and prefer to buy expensive, tasteful, elegant clothes than to wear funky or flashy ones.

## Your Careers

You may work as a lawyer, arbitrator, counselor, designer, decorator, personnel officer, or restaurateur.

## Your Friends and Foes

- You appreciate logical and intelligent people who are also attractive, amusing and successful. You enjoy the company of independent people and those who can take care of you.
- You cannot stand scruffy, loud and coarse types.

## Love and Sex

You can be one of the sexiest members of the zodiac and you are incredibly experimental when you are in the mood. However, you are fussy about your sexual partners and you would prefer to go without sex than to jump into bed with just anybody. If you find the right partner, you will stay with them, although you may not always be faithful to them. Many of you try marriage a couple of times and then end up living happily alone.

## Success in Love and Compatibility

### Libra with Aries

This is a common combination that succeeds over the long term. Libra's laid-back attitude works well with Aries energy and you don't usually compete in the same areas of life.

### Libra with Taurus

You have so much in common that this is a very comfortable arrangement. You both like to feed and entertain others, so your home will be a happy and sociable place.

### Libra with Gemini

You are able to put Gemini's mind at ease, so this can be a pleasant and easygoing combination. You both love to socialize so you can expect life to be full of fun.

### Libra with Cancer

Cancer may be too clinging for your taste and also too prone to bring other family members into every corner of your life.

### Libra with Leo

This can be an extremely passionate partnership, but you love to argue and Leo takes things to heart, while you think a row is nothing more than verbal aerobics.

## Libra with Virgo

Your flirtatious nature may put Virgo on edge and Virgo's fussiness may get you down. This would take a good deal of work.

## Libra with Libra

Oddly enough, Librans can be quite different than each other, so there can be enough to keep you interested. If you are too alike, then you would be better as friends than lovers.

## Libra with Scorpio

Scorpio is too possessive for your tastes and your tendency to flirt will put Scorpio on edge in a big way. You could enjoy a passionate short-term affair.

## Libra with Sagittarius

There may be an initial attraction, but this wears off fairly quickly because you are both apt to drift away and to become involved with other people.

## Libra with Capricorn

This is a good business partnership but Capricorn will get on your nerves on a personal level after a while.

## Libra with Aquarius

This can be a very successful relationship, as neither of you seeks to possess the other. You both love to talk things over and to discuss politics or ideas, so there would be friendship along with a strong sexual link.

### Libra with Pisces

This might make a fun affair, but neither of you are likely to stay around for long, as other attractions could prove irresistible.

## Your Possessions

### Money Attitudes

You can go without if you have to, but you usually ensure that you don't have to. Your innate sense of style means that you are inexorably drawn to the nicest and most expensive item in the shop.

### The Gifts You Most Appreciate

You love beauty and luxury so good clothes, something attractive for the home or nice cosmetics would please you. Ladies would appreciate a day out at a health and beauty center, followed by a visit to a hairdresser. Males enjoy good-looking status symbols, such as a good briefcase, desk set or a smart watch. Artistic ornaments and craft items appeal to you and you love to be given something expensive and stylish to wear.

### Your Favorite Automobile

Given half a chance, you definitely go for something that you cannot afford like a large and fast Jaguar. You are more concerned with the appearance of the vehicle and its state of internal cleanliness than the type of engine that it has.

### Your Ideal Home

Large rooms without too much clutter. Elegant refined decor with clever and decorative ornaments. You must have music playing in most of the rooms. If you can put on an extension for the children and your other relatives that would be great, otherwise you are careful whom you invite to stay.

## Entertainments

### *Your Preferred Drink*

You enjoy sophisticated drinks such as cocktails, good wines, and Southern Comfort. Some Librans are fond of seeking out traditional ales and beers.

### *Your Favorite Meal Out*

You enjoy dining out at posh, expensive, impressive surroundings with music playing in the background. Many Librans enjoy interesting, novel, and very spicy foods.

### *Your Night Out*

You enjoy a meal out with friends where you can enjoy good gossip.

## Your Preferred Activities

You enjoy making love, watching television, eating out, and taking vacations in nice places.

### *Television Preferences*

You prefer to be out and about than watching television but if you do watch, you may prefer a biography, a dramatized documentary, a romantic film, or something about your own special interests.

### The Books You Enjoy

You may prefer watching television to reading. However, you do like magazines and newspapers because you like to keep up with whatever is going on in the world. Picture books appeal and anything romantic or that is about your special interest.

### The Music You Enjoy

You love clever pop music and melodic music. You may also like certain types of jazz and light classical music.

### The Games and Sports That You Enjoy

You might play golf, tennis, lawn bowls, aerobics, dancing, and flying light aircraft.

## Money and Luck

### Your Lucky Number

Seven.

### Your Money Luck

Despite the fact that you are not a notably hard worker, you can be extremely successful in your career, and this brings money your way. Otherwise, your family will help you out when you need money and you can also marry someone who earns or has money.

# Your Karmic Lesson

To take people as they are and to mediate between those who are in dispute. Your role is to be a peacemaker and to have an easy, comfortable life if at all possible.

## Your Correspondences

| Best Day | Friday: this is traditionally Venus's day. |
|---|---|
| Worst Day | Wednesday. |
| Colors | Sky blue, leaf green and pink. |
| Herbs | Mint and aloe. |
| Tissue Salts | Sodium Phosphate. Potassium Phosphate. |
| Aromatherapy Essence | Bergamot. |
| Bach Flower Remedy | Olive. |
| Trees | Cypress. |
| Flowers | Roses. |
| Animals | Rabbit, small deer and the pelican. |
| Metal | Copper. The colors for Venus are pink and green, and copper is an attractive, pink-collared metal that turns green when it oxidizes (rusts). Copper is made from malachite, a deep green stone. |
| Gems | There a number of gems associated with your sign including the sapphire, emerald and also jade. |

# Everything
# Scorpio

8

*(October 24—November 21)*

## Your Element—Water

This is the element of emotion and you are certainly sensitive and emotional. Your feelings run deep but you can also allow your emotions to spill over into areas of your life where logic would serve you better. You can make decisions on the spur of the moment that are based on your feelings at the time, and this can lead you to regret those decisions later in life.

## Your Quality—Fixed

Your fixed nature means that it takes you a while before you find the right partner, the right job or the right place to live, but once you have done so you stick to your choices as hard as you can. Sometimes you hang on too long when it would be better to let things go and this can bring you pain in the long run.

## Your Ruling Planet—Pluto

Pluto, the Roman god of the underworld, is associated with great wealth, most of which is hidden underground. Pluto also rules union with others, birth, death and sex. Before Pluto was discovered, Scorpio was assigned to Mars, the red planet associated with the Roman god of war.

## Your Symbol—the Scorpion

The scorpion once made the mistake of stinging the giant, Orion, who threw him into the sky where he now occupies an area as far as he could possibly be from the constellation of Orion. The scorpion turns its sting onto itself if it feels threatened. The ancient symbol for your sign was once the eagle. This denotes the higher side of Scorpio, which can soar above everything that is base, coarse and petty.

## Your Appearance

There are various types of Scorpio appearances that range from small to medium height, a slim figure and a strong bone structure. Others can run to fat and have a wide face with very widely spaced eyes.

## Your Part of the Body

The sexual organs, the lower stomach, lower spine, the groin, blood, and eyes.

## Your Potential Health Problems

The sexual organs, the stomach and digestive system, lower spine, groin, blood disorders, eye problems, crossed eyes, etc. There can be sudden unexplained paralysis.

## Your Strengths and Weaknesses

### Your Good Bits

You have great endurance, tenacity, and self-control and your strong willpower will overcome almost anything. You are very caring and protective toward your family, especially your partner.

### Your Bad Bits

You can be secretive, suspicious, inflexible, vindictive, and ruthless.

### Your Weaknesses

You are prone to self-destruction, violence, moodiness, clannishness. You love to eat and you may occasionally overdo it where sweet foods and chocolate are concerned. Most of you hate to be out of control, so when you use alcohol, it is usually in moderation.

## Your Favorable Locales

### Cities

Brisbane, Liverpool, Milwaukee, New Orleans, Washington DC.

### Countries

Brazil, Norway, Syria, Zimbabwe.

### Vacations

You are too restless to sit about on a beach for long. A sea cruise probably appeals because you love the sea and you enjoy waking up in new places every day.

### Landscapes

You love being on or by the sea and by lakes and rivers. You also enjoy high places or hot and humid areas. Many Scorpios love deserts.

## Your Foods

Scorpios are supposed to like hot and spicy foods but our experience is that you have delicate stomachs so you prefer plain and ordinary foods like fish or meat and two vegetables. Fried food upsets you. Traditional astrology suggests peppers and leeks. We suggest that you hold the peppers and go for the leeks instead.

## Your Style

You love to shock, so you could turn up looking like Cher in one of her more outrageous outfits. Otherwise, both sexes like wearing casual clothes such as jeans and colorful shirts.

## Your Careers

You need a meaningful job so you may go in for some form of teaching, training or counseling. Many Scorpios work in the medical field, especially as surgeons, but some join the police or get involved with post mortem and forensic work. Other traditionally Scorpio careers are psychiatrist, butcher, miner, and engineer.

## Your Friends and Foes

- Your friends are people who are not afraid of you and who are as passionate about life as you are.
- You have contempt for timid people and you may be uncomfortable around aloof and pretentious people.

# Love and Sex

Scorpios are intense and when you fall in love, your feelings run deep and true. Sex is vital to your health and happiness and you can take this to extremes when the mood hits you.

## Success in Love and Compatibility

### Scorpio with Aries

An extremely hot sexual union, but there would also be many arguments, as each tries to dominate the other. You would soon resort to emotional blackmail to get your own way.

### Scorpio with Taurus

Shared interests make this a good combination as long as you are ready to settle down, otherwise you might find Taurus too quiet for your taste and could become bored and restless.

### Scorpio with Gemini

You both like to talk and discuss things, so this would work well as a friendship, but as a long term love relationship, you would dominate Gemini, making your partner depressed and unhappy.

### Scorpio with Cancer

You both act on gut feelings rather than logic; fine as long as you are singing the same song, otherwise you'll find yourselves out of tune.

### Scorpio with Leo

This either works very well or not at all. At best, both of you are playful and both love a bit of drama and fun in life. Sexually, this could be great fun but it may not work out in the long run.

## Scorpio with Virgo

Both of you are extremely critical and you are both touchy. You could end up resenting each other, which is not a good prospect for a long-term relationship.

## Scorpio with Libra

You need a partner who will make a deep and abiding commitment to the relationship, and Libra finds that extremely difficult. Your arguments could be memorable, but the long-term outlook is not good.

## Scorpio with Scorpio

This would either be a marriage made in heaven or one that ends in hell! It might be fun in the short term, but you are too alike for comfort.

## Scorpio with Sagittarius

You are so different in your approach to life that it would be a difficult match. Sagittarius needs to be free, whereas you can be possessive.

## Scorpio with Capricorn

Capricorn likes to take decisions, and as long as they are sensible ones, you will go along with them most of the time. Capricorn can stand up to you, so it could work well for both of you.

## Scorpio with Aquarius

Both signs are extremely obstinate and tense, so this would very likely become a real battleground. Furthermore, you make decisions as a result of gut feeling, while Aquarius is logical and long-winded.

### Scorpio with Pisces

Both emotional and intuitive, so as long as you have plenty of shared interests, you can get along very well. You may have to take most of the responsibility in this relationship, as Pisces often needs practical help.

## Your Possessions

### Money Attitudes

Your moods control the way you spend or save money at any one point in time and this can make you difficult to understand and to live with. You can go through periods of the most amazing parsimony and then spend money as though it is going out of fashion.

### The Gifts You Most Appreciate

You hate anything that is cheap so any gift, however small, should be of the highest quality. You love music so CDs or tickets to a musical or pop event would delight you. Nice clothes or something attractive for the home always goes down well, as does aftershave, perfume, or good jewelry. Scorpio men love knives, so a clever Swiss army knife would be appreciated. Sports or photographic equipment is also appreciated.

### Your Favorite Automobile

You need a big, fast, powerful limo with tinted windows and plenty of gadgets. An ejector seat for irritating passengers would be nice.

### Your Ideal Home

You would go crazy in a small apartment because you need space and the sight of trees, fields, and landscapes. You need room for your hobbies and interests and for all your books.

## Entertainments

### Your Preferred Drink

Scorpios either drink a great deal or practically nothing at all. Many of you enjoy whisky, especially malt whiskey.

### Your Favorite Meal Out

Your stomach is sensitive, so spicy foods and anything that is unfamiliar is not liked. Many Scorpios enjoy eating soup, either the thin kind with a little pasta added or a thick country broth.

### Your Night Out

Some male Scorpios enjoy lap dancing or strip clubs while others prefer something more refined such as a concert, musical or a pop concert. You love to entertain friends and family in a pub, club, or restaurant.

## Your Preferred Activities

You love to travel, but you also enjoy spending money on indulgent things that you can't normally afford. This could include CDs or spending time luxuriating in a health spa. Many of you also enjoy swimming, diving, caving, and playing team sports and games.

### Television Preferences

You enjoy watching any kind of sport, including motor racing. Documentary programs appeal—also adventures and all those detective programs.

### The Books You Enjoy

Factual and history books, especially about wars and exciting times and also war and spy stores, thrillers and novels with an occult theme.

### The Music You Enjoy

Classical, some pop, also country and western music.

### The Games and Sports That You Enjoy

You love to watch or play tough sports such as rugby, American football, soccer, rough team games, boxing, swimming, caving, swordplay, shooting, and fishing. In short, anything where you can really stretch your body, bludgeon others, or try to kill something!

## Money and Luck

### Your Lucky Number

Eight.

### Your Money Luck

Mainly you earn what you need and you may also provide for others, but you can inherit money, property, or goods from other family members.

# Your Karmic Lesson

Your role is to cope with partners in private and business life, and to care for the needs of weak people or animals.

# Your Correspondences

| | |
|---|---|
| Best Day | Tuesday. Tuesday is traditionally assigned to the Roman god Mars, your sign's ancient ruler. |
| Worst Day | Friday. |
| Colors | Dark red, dark purple. |
| Herbs | Basil. |
| Tissue Salts | Ferrous Phosphate. Calcium Sulphate. Calcium Phosphate. |
| Aromatherapy Essence | Ylang Ylang. |
| Bach Flower Remedy | Impatiens. |
| Trees | Blackthorn, hawthorn, any thorny bush or tree, possibly something like acacia. |
| Flowers | Rhododendron, dark red flowers, cacti. |
| Animals | Scorpion, eagle, shark, mule and snake. |
| Metal | Iron is associated with Mars, the ancient ruler of Scorpio. Iron has a low melting point and it oxidizes (rusts) to a reddish color. These days, plutonium has been added as a Scorpio metal, but it isn't recommended to wear this as jewelry! |
| Gems | Opal, obsidian, onyx, jet, marcasite. |

# Everything
# Sagittarius

*(November 22–December 21)*

**9**

## Your Element—Fire

Fire signs are called the initiators of the zodiac because they don't allow the grass to grow under their feet. If a job needs to be done, there is nobody who can do it more quickly and efficiently than you, but if the job is a long-winded one that requires persistence, you may have to find someone else to come in and finish it. You grasp opportunities when they are offered and you don't understand those who don't have the courage and initiative to do the same themselves. Your intelligence and courage are to be admired but you can become arrogant and overbearing to those who you consider less able than you. You can be a spendthrift, but you are as likely to spend money on others as on yourself.

## Your Quality—Mutable

You are able to adapt fairly easily to new circumstances and you appreciate a change of scenery from time to time. You don't have a very strong personality, so you are happiest when living and working with people who nurture you and who make you feel good about yourself. You love your family but you need to get away and spend a little time alone on occasion in order to recharge your emotional batteries.

## Your Ruling Planet—Jupiter

Jupiter (Jove) was the king of the Roman gods. He was jolly and jovial most of the time, but when he was in a temper, he hurled thunderbolts down on those who angered him.

## Your Symbol—the Archer or the Centaur

The king of the centaurs was a noted archer called Chiron. He taught the Greek heroes Hercules, Theseus and Jason, not only how to shoot straight, but also how to heal. Jupiter placed him among the stars when after an accident which he was wounded and unable to heal himself.

## Your Appearance

Although there are small Sagittarians, you are probably tall and well built, even a little on the heavy side. Your body is usually one of two types, either with large arms and chest and a slim lower half or a small top and large hips and thighs.

## Your Part of the Body

Sagittarius rules the hips and thighs and also the circulation through the legs.

## Your Potential Health Problems

Your weak spots are your hips and thighs and also the circulation through the legs. Your liver, pituitary gland, and some parts of the circulatory system may be sensitive.

## Your Strengths and Weaknesses

### Your Good Bits

You have a wonderful sense of humor and are intelligent, honest, and optimistic. Your values are spiritual rather than materialistic.

### Your Bad Bits

You can be tactless, unrealistic and blind to the truth where it concerns yourself. You also talk about doing things without actually getting around to them or barge ahead and get into a muddle.

### Your Weaknesses

Traveling, making new friends and forgetting your old ones.

You love wine and you may overdo your consumption from time to time. You may enjoy trying exotic or ethnic foods and fast food. Alternatively, you can be a fussy eater, only able to cope with a small range of foods.

## Your Favorable Locales

### Cities

Archangel, Bradford (USA), Budapest, Cologne, Dallas, Haines (Canada), Toledo, Tucson, Wellington.

### Countries

Australia, Hungary, Madagascar, the "cowboy country" in the west of the USA.

### Vacations

You are the great explorer of the zodiac, so you may want to climb remote mountains or journey up the Orinoco. If not, you would enjoy a holiday that allowed you to play golf, windsurf, ski, ride horses, or try your hand at parasailing. Some Sagittarians appreciate the exciting exploration of a deck chair and a good book.

## Landscapes

Farming areas where horses and cattle are kept in addition to open moorland.

## Your Foods

Traditional astrology suggests that you like fruit, currents, asparagus, and tomatoes. You probably eat most things but certain things, such as sugar or acid foods seem to upset you.

## Your Style

You prefer casual clothes for everyday life and really eccentric outfits when you feel like dressing up. You may choose to wear everything in one strange color, such as mauve or orange.

## Your Careers

Many Sagittarians float around for years until they find the right niche. Most love to teach write and to broadcast, so there are many in the media. Your strongly spiritual side can lead you into a religious organization or into spiritualism and spirit healing. You could also work as a publisher or a lawyer or in some aspect of the travel trade, even as a safari guide.

## Your Friends and Foes

- Friends must have a sense of humor and not be too critical.
- You cannot stand pretentious or very serious people or those who use their intelligence to take advantage of others.

## Love and Sex

You need freedom within a relationship or to be free of perma-
nent ties altogether and the chances are that you are a better
friend than you are a partner. Sexually you are probably ready
to try anything once—or more than once if possible. Some
Sagittarians are far more conventional in both their attitude to
love and to sex.

## *Success in Love and Compatibility*

### Sagittarius with Aries

You both do everything at the speed of light, so you don't irritate each other. You need more patience than Aries can muster,
although you would become good friends.

### Sagittarius with Taurus

You have so little in common that it is hard to see how you could
stay interested in each other over the long term. An initial attraction of opposites might make for a pleasant fling though.

### Sagittarius with Gemini

You share a great sense of humor and a desire to get out and
see new people and places. You enjoy each other's company and
share many interests, so this could be a successful relationship.

### Sagittarius with Cancer

Cancer loves home life and to have the family, parents, children
and in-laws around, while you need freedom, space and time to
think. We can't see this working in the long run.

## Sagittarius with Leo

Competitiveness and arguments could mar an otherwise good match, but a short fling or a friendship might work, even though a long-term relationship would be hard to maintain.

## Sagittarius with Virgo

You share a great sense of humor, but Virgo values hard work while you prefer an easy life, so you may have to accept that one of you will earn the bread and butter for both of you.

## Sagittarius with Libra

Both of you live in dreamland half the time, so as long as you can earn enough to keep the home from falling apart, you can drift and dream together.

## Sagittarius with Scorpio

Scorpio is possessive and far too interested in what is going on in your mind for comfort. You share an interest in travel, so as friends you can get on quite well together, for a while at least.

## Sagittarius with Sagittarius

You either get on famously together or you soon find yourselves becoming irritated by your similarities. Neither of you like long term relationships much, so it may not last.

## Sagittarius with Capricorn

You could find Capricorn's ambition hard to cope with but as long as you allow your partner to get on with earning the money while you plan trips and outings it could work.

### Sagittarius with Aquarius

You are both independent and intelligent so you would certainly become good friends. Your shared interest in sexual experimentation could help to cement the relationship.

### Sagittarius with Pisces

This could be an extremely successful relationship if you happen to share spiritual interests. If you don't, then you won't have enough in common deep down, where it really matters

## Your Possessions

### Money Attitudes

How you get by is a mystery to us all! You studiously avoid doing anything the least bit sensible with your money, but you have the luck of the Irish when it comes to winning money, marrying it, or just finding it when you most need it.

### The Gifts You Most Appreciate

You have an offbeat sense of humor so you appreciate anything that is quirky or different. An interesting ornament that reflects your special interests would please you. If you are able to care for a pet, you might appreciate a tank full of tropical fish or a pet snake! Otherwise, a sporty backpack, wheeled luggage, dramatic jewelry, or a garish sweater covered in sequins!

### Your Favorite Automobile

You are happy with anything that gets you from A to B. You may drive about in something large and scruffy that has plenty of character, like an old pick-up or an old van that has been customized with your favorite paint-spray can. A motorcycle may suit your needs.

## Your Ideal Home

You prefer a home in the country where there is plenty of space around. If this is also near water, so much the better but you also need to be able to get into town to visit interesting shops from time to time. You need space for your hobbies and your collection of interesting odds and ends.

# Entertainments

## Your Preferred Drink

You probably quaff large quantities of wine or ale until your stomach or liver start to complain.

## Your Favorite Meal Out

You either like exotic and interesting food or something bland such as pasta or a traditional kind of meal.

## Your Night Out

Anything that has a sporting or competitive element would suit you, so you might go to a basketball game, a boxing match, or you may take your friends skating.

# Your Preferred Activities

Fishing, swimming, exploring and wandering around the shops.

### Television Preferences

Your attention span is so short that you probably only concentrate on commercials! You prefer to be out than at home watching TV.

### The Books You Enjoy

Tourist guides to exotic places, or nonfiction books on spiritualty or mundane matters. You also enjoy fantasy and science fiction.

### The Music You Enjoy

Amusing music with funny lyrics appeals to you. Otherwise, pretty standard pop, rock music, and country and western tunes.

### The Games and Sports That You Enjoy

Sagittarians are supposed to love the outdoor life and to be especially interested in horse riding or horse racing. This may not necessarily be so but you would enjoy team games or golf, tennis or archery in a nice country club atmosphere. If in town, you might enjoy squash or aerobics in an expensive leisure center.

## Money and Luck

### Your Lucky Number

Nine.

### Your Money Luck

Nobody is luckier than a Sagittarian, so you can expect more than a few windfalls in your life or wins on raffles, lotteries, and so on.

## Your Karmic Lesson

Your job seems to be to learn through some form of suffering and to allow your soul to grow so that you can have a better incarnation the next time around.

## Your Correspondences

| | |
|---|---|
| Best Day | Thursday. Thursday is associated with the Roman god Jupiter. |
| Worst Day | Saturday. |
| Colors | Royal blue and imperial purple. |
| Herbs | Aniseed. |
| Tissue Salts | Ferrous Phosphate. Sodium Sulphate. Silica. |
| Aromatherapy Essence | Rosemary. |
| Bach Flower Remedy | Vervain. |
| Trees | Oak, lime, mulberry, ash, and birch. |
| Flowers | Dandelion, pinks, rushes, and the pimpernel. |
| Animals | Sheep, stag, elephant, tiger, and horse. |
| Metal | Tin. |
| Gems | There are various gems associated with your sign, including the topaz, carbuncle, and sapphire. |

# Everything
# Capricorn
*(December 22–January 19)*

**10**

## Your Element—Earth

You are practical, diligent, hard working and often happiest when doing something useful. You can be relied upon even though it might take you a while to get around to things. You are thorough and capable, but you can't stand being harassed or rushed. You have a creative streak and your sensuality means that you know how to make things (and people) look and feel good. Being shrewd and cautious, you need material and emotional security and you will put up with a lot in order to get it and then to keep hold of it. You may appear stingy to outsiders but this is because you fear future poverty. You cling to your family, but being sociable, you don't usually keep outsiders at a distance.

## Your Quality—Cardinal

There is a kind of self-centeredness about all cardinal sign people, which means that it is hard to push you into doing things that you don't wish to do. You can come up with some great ideas but you may not always be able to carry them through to their logical conclusion. You take responsibility easily and you can care for those who are weaker than yourself, but if others try to hold you back, you will resist.

## Your Ruling Planet—Saturn

This rather gloomy Roman god represents limitations and hard lessons in life but the musical and cheerful god, Pan, is also associated with Capricorn.

## Your Symbol—the Goat

This sign is said to represent the mythical goat, Amalthea, which suckled Jupiter in his infancy. Playfully, the baby god pulled off one of its horns, which then became the Cornucopia or horn of plenty. The merry, goat-footed god, Pan, is also associated with this sign. The mountain goat climbs onward and upward in a sure-footed Capricorn manner.

## Your Appearance

You are most likely slim and medium in height. Your bone structure is good and this stands you in good stead when you get older—you tend to have an ageless appearance.

## Your Part of the Body

Capricorn rules the skin, ears, bones, knees, and teeth. This sign is also associated with chronic ailments such as rheumatism.

## Your Potential Health Problems

The knees are especially vulnerable as are the bones and skin, ears and teeth. You may suffer with problems associated with the gall bladder, digestion, and the spleen. Capricorn is associated with chronic ailments such as rheumatism, asthma and eczema.

## Your Strengths and Weaknesses

### Your Good Bits

You work hard, look after your family and you have a sense

of duty. You also have a good sense of humor and you can be sociable and great fun when you are in the right mood. You are realistic.

## Your Bad Bits

You can be dull and dry, stingy and lacking in imagination.

## Your Weaknesses

You are ambitious, and while this is kept in proportion, it is all well and good, but you may forget the needs of those around you. You like status symbols and a comfortable lifestyle but you are prepared to work for this. You may be stingy and also prone to depression.

You may overdo the junk food and snacks or even go without food at times when your heavy workload makes it impossible for you to eat properly. Your sign is not noted for drinking much alcohol, but you like a shot of whisky or a cocktail with friends as a pleasant interlude.

# Your Favorable Locales

## Cities

Brussels, Delhi, Hartford, Mexico City, Rio de Janeiro, Saint John (Canada).

## Countries

Afghanistan, the Balkans, India, Lithuania, Mexico, the West Indies.

## Vacations

You are fond of traveling and you like to take some fairly gentle exercise. Therefore, a holiday by the sea, offering an opportunity to go sailing or walking, might suit you.

## Landscapes

High mountains (remember the symbol of the goat), rock, and snow.

# Your Foods

You were probably taught to eat up your dinner and not to waste food when you were small. You probably still eat more or less what is put in front of you and you are unlikely to be a fussy eater.

# Your Style

When young, you prefer fairly formal clothes of good quality and made to last. When you get older, you become a bit more adventurous and happy to try out different colors and styles.

# Your Careers

You are attuned to a professional career with accountancy and banking being high on the list. However, any kind of large business would attract you, especially if the job included detailed work and didn't require you to be hurried. You may also choose to be a dentist, doctor, lawyer, or property dealer. Yours is the scientific sign so some form of scientific research or collation of evidence might suit you.

## Your Friends and Foes

- You respect people who are loyal, hard working and fair, but you are closest to your family, and friends come a long way behind them.
- You can't tolerate feckless or stupid people who ignore authority.

## Love and Sex

You are cautious about the people you choose to love, and you don't like to move from one partner to another. You may reserve most of your love for your parents and other family members. Sexually, you can be slightly experimental, but for the most part, you prefer to stick to the tried and tested.

### Success in Love and Compatibility

#### Capricorn with Aries

You are both capable, hard working, and ambitious. While Aries is politically adroit, you have common sense. You can enjoy a happy and productive life together as long as you have shared goals.

#### Capricorn with Taurus

You understand each other's needs and priorities, and you go at the same pace as each other, so this can be a perfect match.

#### Capricorn with Gemini

The only things you have in common are fussiness and a tendency to martyr yourselves for your families. An unusual but occasionally successful union.

### Capricorn with Cancer

Your attitudes to family life, money and business are extremely similar, so you can make a real go of this. However, it works best when Cancer is the homemaker and Capricorn the worker.

### Capricorn with Leo

This is an extremely competitive partnership with both of you striving to be the boss. You would try to restrict Leo in some way and this is would be a losing battle.

### Capricorn with Virgo

You see life from similar points of view and share many characteristics in common. As long as you don't both sink into dullness and depression, you can have a happy life together.

### Capricorn with Libra

Some Capricorns are sociable and outgoing and if you are one of these, you and your Libran partner would have a lot of fun together. You will be happy to work hard while Libra spends money so elegantly.

### Capricorn with Scorpio

There is no reason on earth why this should work, but it often does. It is as if you each supply the missing parts of each other's natures, and Scorpio will help you to achieve your ambitions.

### Capricorn with Sagittarius

This would be a difficult love relationship, but possibly a happy working one, as Sagittarius would bring enthusiasm to the venture.

### Capricorn with Capricorn

Not all Capricorns are alike but your basic beliefs and priorities will be the same, so there will be enough in common and enough that is different to create some kind of spark. If you are too alike though, the spark will be too feeble to last.

### Capricorn with Aquarius

Aquarius suffers from foot-in-mouth syndrome and you take offense at everything—this won't last past the initial attraction.

### Capricorn with Pisces

You are dutiful and organized while Pisces is intuitive, romantic, mystical, and totally disorganized. This might be an interesting short term affair for you both, but it won't stand the test of time.

## Your Possessions

### Money Attitudes

Being broke is just not your style. The chances are that your parents didn't have much to spare and you learned to be sensible, to work hard for your money, and then conserve what you have. Take care that your fear of poverty doesn't turn you into a miser.

### The Gifts You Most Appreciate

A computer or some office machinery might please you, as would tools or a musical instrument. You find it hard to indulge yourself, so anything luxurious would suit you. A smart briefcase or desk set might suit males while nice clothes or a trip to a spa would please women. A night out with dinner and dancing would be nice too. You would appreciate a nice clock or watch, mono-grammed stationery, CD's, or electronics.

## Your Favorite Automobile

You would probably enjoy owning some kind of all-weather and all-terrain vehicle, such as a jeep or a British Land-Rover. You probably complain about the running costs. Otherwise, an executive limo would suit you.

## Your Ideal Home

If possible, you would choose to live in a warm country, other-wise a home with excellent central heating. You can live in an apartment, but you would need to get out of it often to indulge in your hobbies and interests. You prefer to have your family close by and also to have them drop in on you as often as possible. You would be luckiest when living high up on a hill or a mountain.

# Entertainments

## Your Preferred Drink

You probably don't like wasting money on alcohol, but when you do drink, you prefer a small glass of brandy, good wine, or a liqueur.

## Your Favorite Meal Out

Capricorns enjoy good food, well cooked and presented and at a reasonable price. You may enjoy curries and spicy foods.

## Your Night Out

You love to dance and you enjoy upbeat music, so you might like ballroom dancing, old time dancing, line dancing, Latin American dancing, or anything else of the kind. You may even take exams and become quite professional. Other outings would include picnics and music in the park type of events.

## Your Preferred Activities

You probably like to work as much as anything else, but you can be equally happy decorating your house. When you do relax, it will be by doing things with your family or playing with your pets.

### Television Preferences

You probably enjoy recording your favorite programs; otherwise, you have no special favorites. You may enjoy the soaps.

### The Books You Enjoy

You enjoy reading novels that give you something to think about and discuss with your partner. You like newspapers and magazines.

### The Music You Enjoy

The blues, classical music, and music that you can dance to.

### The Games and Sports That You Enjoy

Many Capricorns love to dance, and also enjoy climbing. Team sports are not really your thing. Board games that have a mathematic, financial, or strategic element to them may please you.

## Money and Luck

### Your Lucky Number

Ten.

## Your Money Luck

You work for what you get and sometimes it is a long time coming. You have better luck in old age than when you are young.

## Your Karmic Lesson

You will always work hard and look after your family and close friends. You may be too dutiful and austere, so you should learn to lighten up.

## Your Correspondences

| | |
|---|---|
| Best Day | Saturday. This is the day associated with the Roman god, Saturn. Literally, Saturn's day. |
| Worst Day | Thursday. |
| Colors | Black, grey, dark green, mustard and brown. |
| Herbs | Sage and sorrel. |
| Tissue Salts | Calcium Phosphate. Silica. Potassium Chloride. |
| Aromatherapy Essence | Coriander. |
| Bach Flower Remedy | Elm. |
| Trees | Yew. |
| Flowers | Pansy, hemlock, ivy and thistle. |
| Animals | Goat, donkey, elephant and toad. |
| Metal | Lead. |
| Gems | There are a number of gems associated with your sign, including the turquoise, black opal and tourmaline. |

# Everything
# Aquarius

*(January 20—February 18)*

## Your Element—Air

Yours is the element of communication, so you will always choose a job and a lifestyle that keeps you in touch with others and probably also one that takes you from one place to another. You need a variety of interests in your life and plenty of places to go and people to see. You may spend more on the phone than is healthy for your bank balance but it keeps you sane, so what the heck! Your mind is quick and you can often see solutions to other people's problems, although you are less able to solve your own problems when they arise.

## Your Quality—Fixed

Your fixed nature means that it takes you a while before you find the right partner, the right job, or the right place to live, but once you have done so you stick to your choices as hard as you can. Sometimes you hang on too long when it would be better to let things go and this can bring you pain in the long run.

## Your Ruling Planet—Uranus

This planet behaves very differently from all the others in the solar system as its poles are at its east and west and it revolves in a different direction from all the other planets. Therefore, astrologers consider that it represents unpredictable behavior and eccentricity. Before the discovery of Uranus, Saturn was considered to be the ruler of Aquarius.

## Your Symbol—the Water Carrier

This confuses beginners in astrology as they invariably link the Water Carrier symbol to the element of water, but as we have already seen, Aquarius is actually an air sign. The Water Carrier represents a reservoir of knowledge. Other aspects of this deep symbol include a cloud of water that is carried through the air. This is a frightening symbol for people born during the 20th century because it carries images of nuclear fallout and of course, uranium is associated with Aquarius.

## Your Appearance

Most Aquarians are average to tall in height and they have a high forehead, which is accentuated in men because their hairline often recedes fairly early in life. The eyes are often quite magnetic, the expression is serious and they speak slowly. Other Aquarians are short and overweight with thick wavy hair and they are altogether quicker in everything than the other type.

## Your Part of the Body

Aquarius rules the ankles and circulation to the extremities and also breathing.

## Your Potential Health Problems

Your weak points are the ankles and circulation to the extremities, also your breathing. This sign is also associated with cramps and nervous breakdowns.

## Your Strengths and Weaknesses

### Your Good Bits

You are friendly, independent and talented and you have an excellent mind.

### Your Bad Bits

It is hard for you to get in touch with your own emotions. You rebel against authority and you can be eccentric and as vague as an absent-minded professor.

### Your Weaknesses

Your ability to argue logically and endlessly would impress Mr. Spock or any other Vulcan.

You are not a fussy eater and you like a wide range of foods, but you particularly enjoy tasty dishes such as Chinese or Thai foods. You also love salty snacks, olives and pickles, as well as cookies and fruitcake. You need to watch your salt and sugar intake as these can cause an imbalance.

## Your Favorable Locales

### Cities

Bremen, Brighton, Dayton, Halifax (Canada), Hamburg, Lubbock, Miami, Moscow, Salisbury, Toronto.

### Countries

Ethiopia, Russia, Sweden.

## Vacations

You like places which are interesting and which also offer good quality food and accommodation. You would probably enjoy a visit to the Kennedy Space Center in Florida. Aquarians cannot really be categorized, but generally speaking, you are not great travelers.

## Landscapes

You enjoy natural, uncultivated places and open, hilly areas with good views and wonderful light. You also love to be by the sea.

## Your Foods

Most Aquarians are pretty easy to cater for but some are vegetarian due to a dislike of killing and eating animals. Some can be faddy in other ways too.

## Your Style

Aquarians are so individual that it is impossible to categorize your style but one thing seems to be shared by all of you: a dislike of wearing the kind of suits that office workers usually have to wear. You may choose clothes that are stylish, casual, or totally individual and quite eccentric. You hate fussy clothes and formal clothes.

## Your Careers

You like to help people and you have a friendly, nonjudgmental attitude so you can be a teacher, an advisor, an arbitrator, or a lawyer. In addition, you like new technology, so you may go in for computer science, rocketry and some other branch of scientific exploration, or anything else that is unusual. Idealism can lead to a career in a charity organization, but you may also take up astrology or counseling.

## Your Friends and Foes

- You need plenty of friends and they must be clever, kind hearted, interesting and humorous.
- You dislike over-emotional, clingy people who will drain you.

## Love and Sex

Some Aquarians are too independent to stay with anybody for long while others marry young and stay put. If you fall in love, your feelings run deep and you are serious about marriage; if you don't, you can be amazingly casual about the feelings of others. Sex is very important to your sign and you are a generous and inventive lover.

### Success in Love and Compatibility

#### Aquarius with Aries

You can dream up good ideas, while Aries can get things off the ground. You don't object to Aries's flirtatiousness either, so you can get along very well together.

#### Aquarius with Taurus

You are both obstinate and unlikely to see the other's point of view unless you both learn to give way from time to time. You respect Taurus's practicality.

## Aquarius with Gemini

Gemini is better at working and earning money than you are. In addition, you share an interest in sex, so you could have a successful and exciting relationship.

## Aquarius with Cancer

Cancer's clingy nature doesn't fit well with your need for independence. You don't think alike, because you are logical while Cancer jumps to conclusions or acts on intuition and instinct.

## Aquarius with Leo

You can be inspired by Leo and you can be friends who respect one another as well as being lovers. You are both interested in lovemaking, so this also helps the relationship along.

## Aquarius with Virgo

This can just work, as long as Virgo doesn't need too much reassurance and is not too fussy and neurotic. You share a wonderful sense of fun and sense of humor.

## Aquarius with Libra

This can be a good combination as long as neither of you is the argumentative type. You share intellectual interests but you may not share Libra's interest in art and homemaking.

## Aquarius with Scorpio

You are both stubborn and you both tend to think that you are right all the time, so this is not a good match. Scorpio's emotional approach to life will confuse you.

### Aquarius with Sagittarius

This is a fun combination with many shared interests, but you are both independent and neither of you may be in a hurry to make a long-term commitment.

### Aquarius with Capricorn

You have some interests in common but you are idealistic while Capricorn is status-conscious and materialistic, so you could clash.

### Aquarius with Aquarius

There is such variation from one Aquarian to the next that you are all different from each other! This keeps boredom at bay.

### Aquarius with Pisces

Anything can happen in this weird and wonderful match as you are both idealists but you are both impractical so you would need a good accountant to help run your lives.

## Your Possessions

### *Money Attitudes*

Eccentric to the last, your attitude to finances defies all understanding. You know exactly what you should do to save money, but somehow the theory doesn't always translate into practice— especially when a new gadget comes onto the market!

## The Gifts You Most Appreciate

You may be eccentric but you do appreciate a touch of luxury. Therefore, a good quality gift that reflects your special interest would suit you. You may collect china animals, chess sets, Japanese tea sets or Tarot cards, so an addition to your collection would be nice. Another idea would be a reading with a good astrologer. Otherwise, you enjoy bookshelves and plenty of books to put on them, electronic gadgets, and anything to do with computers.

## Your Favorite Automobile

You like a large vehicle with a good engine and plenty of power. You may enjoy a digital dashboard and a computerized illustration of the inside and outside temperature, a moving map, a tracking device for local speed traps, and a wonderful sound system. This space-age machine will either be kept in a pristine state or it will be utterly filthy. You love to have space for all your goods, so a mini-bus would appeal as well.

## Your Ideal Home

Aquarians are so peculiar that it is hard to say how you would choose to live. Some of you like a home full of animals, children, noise, and mess, and others need a spare, cool looking home with loads of space. Some love soft, feminine colors while others would enjoy living with stark, modernistic black and white furnishings. Many of you love the idea of living in an old castle or some other ancient house that is filled with loads of antiques and interesting junk.

## Entertainments

### Your Preferred Drink

You enjoy talking over a drink and a meal with friends, so plenty of red wine, beer, lager or any other type of social drink is acceptable but you rarely drink to excess.

### Your Favorite Meal Out

You may be a vegetarian or a "funny" eater. If not, you enjoy experimenting with ethnic cuisine such as Chinese, Jewish, Italian, Greek, Lebanese, vegetarian, Oriental or any kind of specialized food.

### Your Night Out

Your sign is so unpredictable and so interested in things that are a bit different that you could enjoy a fireworks display and an evening at a fairground, complete with hot dog and mustard. Alternatively, you may love to pamper yourself at a spa, go to an astrology workshop or attend a poetry reading.

## Your Preferred Activities

You enjoy playing gentle sports, chatting with friends, having a Tarot reading or losing yourself in a book.

### Television Preferences

Cartoons, science fiction—you may even be a "Trekkie" or, if British, a "Doctor Who" fan. Documentaries and educational programs are liked, as are interesting plays and murder mysteries or spy stories.

### The Books You Enjoy

Owning books is as important to you as reading them and you encourage your family to do the same. You love to be surrounded by books, newspapers, magazines, pamphlets, and bits of paper with writing on them. To do you justice however, you do try to read everything within your reach and will even read the advertising on a packet of cereal rather than have nothing for your eyes to wander over. Many Aquarians enjoy science fiction and books about interesting and outlandish things such as UFOs.

### The Music You Enjoy

This could be anything from classical to rock music, but you don't much care for background "Muzak." Some of you love jazz or clever synthesizer music, while others are keen on new age music, the sound of a sitar or something equally unusual.

### The Games and Sports That You Enjoy

Word games such as Scrabble and also chess. You probably don't enjoy team games, but golf may appeal, or anything that you can do alone, such as fishing. Many Aquarians like tap or ballroom dancing. Some of you prefer attending interesting seminars (especially astrology ones) and committee meetings to any kind of games or sports.

## Money and Luck

### Your Lucky Number

Eleven.

## *Your Money Luck*

You are fairly sensible where money is concerned, so you will work, save, set up a pension scheme and spend as little as necessary most of the time. You can be lucky with property dealings, especially if you are one of the many Aquarians who likes doing renovations and decorating and then selling or renting out property.

## **Your Karmic Lesson**

You have to learn to get close to others and to avoid becoming isolated. Another lesson is to learn and then to teach and advise others.

## Your Correspondences

| | |
|---|---|
| Best Day | Saturday. Before the planet Uranus was discovered, your ruling planet was Saturn, and Saturday is Saturn's day. |
| Worst Day | Monday. |
| Colors | Neon colors, electric blue, lilac, violet, purple and indigo. |
| Herbs | Your sign is probably more attuned to spices like cumin than herbs but fennel is also associated with Aquarius. |
| Tissue Salts | Sodium Chloride. Ferrous Phosphate. Potassium Phosphate. |
| Aromatherapy Essence | Cypress. |
| Your Bach Flower Remedy | Sweet chestnut. |
| Trees | Willow. |
| Flowers | Orchids, absinthe, buttercup. |
| Animals | Cat, hare, mouse. |
| Metal | These days uranium is considered to be the metal for your sign but lead was the old metal that was associated with Saturn, the old ruler of Aquarius. Platinum is also considered to be an Aquarian metal. |
| Gems | There are two gems associated with your sign. One is lapis lazuli and the other is amethyst. Many Aquarians enjoy buying crystals such as amethyst for meditation or healing purposes. |

# Everything
# Pisces

## 12

*(February 19–March 20)*

## Your Element—Water

This is the element of emotion and you are certainly sensitive and emotional. Your feelings run deep but you can also allow your emotions to spill over into areas of your life where logic would serve you better. You can make decisions on the spur of the moment that are based on your feelings at the time, and this can lead you to regret those decisions later in life.

## Your Quality—Mutable

You are able to adapt fairly easily to new circumstances and you appreciate a change of scenery from time to time. You don't have a very strong personality, so you are happiest when living and working with people who nurture you and who make you feel good about yourself. You love your family but you need to get away and spend a little time alone on occasion in order to recharge your emotional batteries.

## Your Ruling Planet—Neptune

The Roman god, Neptune, ruled the sea and all the mysterious things that are hidden from sight under it. Before Neptune was discovered, your sign was said to be ruled by Jupiter.

## Your Symbol—the Fish

Two fish that are tied together and swimming in different directions are the symbol for your sign. The Babylonians knew the constellation of Pisces as "Kun," which means "the tails." This is very appropriate for the last sign of the zodiac. It was also known as the leash, which was the link between the two fish. The symbol itself may commemorate the occasion when Venus and Cupid disguised themselves as fish in order to escape from an angry giant.

## Your Appearance

You are of middling height and weight or a little on the tall side and you can gain weight later in life. You have a lovely smile and eyes that light up when you laugh. Unfortunately, your features suffer from the weather and from aging, so you might need to use plenty of good products on your face.

## Your Part of the Body

Your sign rules the feet, but also the mind and the psychic and intuitive faculties; it also rules the lungs.

## Your Potential Health Problems

Your weak spots are your feet, lungs and some body fluids. You may have allergic conditions and ailments caused by misuse of drink and drugs. You may suffer from nervous debility, confusion, and peculiar mental states.

## Your Strengths and Weaknesses

### Your Good Bits

You are imaginative, sensitive, creative, and helpful to those who are in pain or difficulty.

### Your Bad Bits

You can be indecisive, inclined to worry over nothing and you find it hard to finish what you start.

### Your Weaknesses

You can muddle along in a chaotic state, avoid making decisions, and sink into escapism by drinking alcohol and taking drugs.

You love to cook and eat and you are not a picky eater, although the animal lovers among you may opt for a vegetarian diet. Alcohol is your real downfall.

## Your Favorable Locales

### Cities

Alexandria, Christchurch, Cincinnati, Norfolk (USA), Regina (Canada), San Diego, Sao Paolo, Seville.

### Countries

New Zealand, Portugal, the Sahara.

### Vacations

You love to be in, on or near the sea. You enjoy sea views and some of you like snorkeling and scuba diving, where you can be, literally, in your element. You would enjoy visiting any area that has a coral reef that you can swim around, or look at through a glass-bottomed boat.

## Landscapes

You appreciate seashores, coastal cliffs, lakes and fast-moving rivers.

# Your Foods

You may be a vegetarian because you may feel that it is wrong to eat the flesh of animals. If you are not too bothered about this, you probably like fish and seafood. You are not a fussy or faddy eater apart from your possible vegetarianism.

# Your Style

Pisceans simply loved the hippy era and the fancy dress of the seventies. Nowadays, you probably prefer jeans or casual clothes in gentle, romantic colors. Some of you are very smart and dressy while others wear whatever comes to hand. You are careful with money, so you can do well by trawling thrift and charity shops. Shoes are your weakness and if you overspend, it is on footwear.

# Your Careers

Any creative or artistic profession suits you, as does any branch of show business. You love to help others, so you can work for a charity or teach, counsel or heal people by working in the medical field or by becoming a spiritual healer. There are numerous

Piscean Tarot card readers, mediums, healers, psychotherapists, teachers and astrologers.

## Your Friends and Foes

- You prefer easygoing people who are sympathetic, good listeners and who have a sense of fun.
- You dislike cold, logical people and heartless ones who are cruel to animals or children. You cannot take to formal or fussy types either.

## Love and Sex

You can be happy in a loving relationship as long as you have the space to be yourself. If someone gives you the third degree about where you are and what time you will be back, it will drive you insane. Sexually, you are prepared to try most things—especially when you have had a few drinks!

### *Success in Love and Compatibility*

**Pisces with Aries**

You share some interests and you may get on well enough to make this last. However, Aries could be too pushy for your taste.

**Pisces with Taurus**

You share an interest in art, music, gardening, the home and family life. Along with a shared sensual nature and an interest in sex, this can be very good.

## Pisces with Gemini

You are both adaptable and you share a sense of humor, but you may be a little too disorganized for Gemini to cope with in the long term, although you could have a pleasant short-term love affair.

## Pisces with Cancer

You are both intuitive and both make decisions by instinct rather than by logic, so you have much in common. You both also enjoy family life, homemaking, and travel.

## Pisces with Leo

As long as Leo is happy to be the one who earns the money and organizes things, this would work well, as you would take care of the home and the family for your partner.

## Pisces with Virgo

With give and take on both sides, this can work well, but you would have to take care not to overburden Virgo. Virgo is happy to take on someone who needs rescuing, but you could rapidly wear out your partner.

## Pisces with Libra

Good sexual rapport but otherwise disappointing as you just do not think the same way that the other does. You can both dither at times so you may never get the relationship off the ground.

### Pisces with Scorpio

As long as the Scorpio is very loving, this can work well because both of you are emotional, sensitive and intuitive. If you share an interest in animals, travel, or sex you would have it made.

### Pisces with Sagittarius

You share a great sense of humor and a love of travel, psychic matters and astrology so you have much in common. If you can both stand a long-term relationship, this would work.

### Pisces with Capricorn

There could be an initial attraction of opposites, but there is so little common ground that this would have very little chance of working out in the long term. Capricorn might be too dull and hard working for your taste.

### Pisces with Aquarius

Neither of you are very practical, but you should get on well in many ways. Aquarius can be stubborn and determined, but you are adaptable—so it could work.

### Pisces with Pisces

You both love a drink and a good laugh. You are both pretty easy-going, so as long as there is enough money in the pot, you will be fine together.

# Your Possessions

## Money Attitudes

Your outlook is spiritual rather than materialistic. When you add this to your generosity to your loved ones and your dislike of the rat race, one can see why you rarely have oodles of cash in the bank.

## The Gifts You Most Appreciate

You appreciate art and a touch of luxury. You would love to choose a lovely painting or artistic object and have someone pay for this for you. Otherwise, you may appreciate fishing tackle, some other sports equipment or a pair of expensive boots.

## Your Favorite Automobile

An astonishing number of Pisceans don't drive at all. Others are very fast drivers who love sports vehicles and other fast automobiles. In addition to your speedy vehicle, you may have a battered old horse trailer or some kind of recreational vehicle.

## Your Ideal Home

You would love to live by the sea or some other source of water. You may have a small apartment in town and a house by the sea. Otherwise, anything unusual such as a converted church or railway station might suit you. Whatever you choose to live in, there must be a hostelry nearby!

## Entertainments

### Your Preferred Drink

Anything really! There are even rumours that there is blood in your alcohol!

### Your Favorite Meal Out

You are probably a good cook, so you can be fairly discriminating about the standard of food and service when you eat out. Oddly enough, you are more likely to complain about the food in a restaurant than many more apparently assertive people would. Many Pisceans are vegetarians, or enjoy fish meals.

### Your Night Out

You enjoy a quiz night in a pub or bar and you love to have a drink and chat with friends. Otherwise, a walk by the sea or in pleasant countryside appeals to you. You may enjoy going to a show or to see your favorite sports team play.

## Your Preferred Activities

Dreaming, being creative and using your imagination. Many Pisceans are very good dancers, despite the fact that they are likely to have two left feet.

### Television Preferences

You enjoy biographies, true-life stories, animal and wildlife programs, romance, sagas and old films of all kinds. You love to laugh so a good comedy will always suit you.

## The Books You Enjoy

You love to read about people, but you also enjoy nonfiction books on your special interest. You read books on natural health therapies and cook books along with newspapers and magazines.

Some of you read about politics or finance, even though you may not involve yourself personally in these things; others read about psychic, fantasy, or mystical subjects.

## The Music You Enjoy

You really understand and appreciate music, so whether it is pop or classical, it must be well performed and, if on CD, the best orchestra and the best quality of recording that you can find.

You might enjoy ballads, ballet music, or something that reminds you of the past. You may like animal-style meditation music with dolphins, birds and whales singing along to the tune (or lack of tune!).

## The Games and Sports That You Enjoy

Oddly enough, Pisceans are quite sporty in various ways. You enjoy walking, aerobics, swimming, and above all, dancing. You love to travel and you may enjoy fishing.

## Money and Luck

### Your Lucky Number

Twelve.

### Your Money Luck

Your money fluctuates wildly and although you are sensible, you can be too generous to your friends and loved ones. You can win on lotteries and raffles, but for the most part, you need to earn and save if you are to get by. Fortunately, you are one of the workers of the zodiac, so you can always earn money when you need to.

## Your Karmic Lesson

You will be called upon to sacrifice something for the sake of others during your lifetime, but you should avoid making a martyr of yourself and allowing others to drain your mental, emotional and financial resources.

# Your Correspondences

| | |
|---|---|
| Best Day | Thursday. The days of the week pre-date the discovery of the outer planets; therefore, your day is Thursday, which is Jupiter's day. |
| Worst Day | Wednesday. |
| Colors | Sea colors, green-blues, turquoise, lavender, lilac and purple. |
| Herbs | You are more attuned to spices than to herbs and cloves is supposed to link with your sign. However, the birthwort, which was supposed to ease the pains of childbirth, is also associated with Pisces. |
| Tissue Salts | Iron Phosphate. Magnesium Phosphate. Silica. Sodium Sulphate. |
| Aromatherapy Essence | Red chestnut. |
| Bach Flower Remedy | Wild rose. |
| Trees | Lime. |
| Flowers | Water lily and poppy. The sign of Pisces is associated with sleep and also escapism through drink and narcotics, therefore the poppy is appropriate. |
| Animals | Fish, dolphin and the mythical unicorn. |
| Metal | Tin. |
| Gems | There are various gems associated with your sign, including the cool, romantic moonstone, the passionate bloodstone, and the pearl. |

# Quick Compatibility Check

**13**

A lthough we cover your attitude to love and sex within the body of this book, this section will provide you a quick guide to the signs that you are most compatible with, as lovers, as friends, and as coworkers.

## Compatibility with Friends and Lovers

| YOUR SIGN | GREAT | GOOD | FAIR | NOPE |
|-----------|-------|------|------|------|
| Aries | Libra | Aquarius | Pisces | Virgo |
| Taurus | Leo | Libra | Capricorn | Sagittarius |
| Gemini | Aries | Virgo | Aquarius | Scorpio |
| Cancer | Capricorn | Taurus | Pisces | Sagittarius |
| Leo | Aquarius | Libra | Virgo | Aries |
| Virgo | Cancer | Gemini | Pisces | Aries |
| Libra | Aries | Gemini | Aquarius | Pisces |
| Scorpio | Leo | Cancer | Taurus | Virgo |
| Sagittarius | Virgo | Capricorn | Pisces | Taurus |
| Capricorn | Scorpio | Cancer | Taurus | Leo |
| Aquarius | Aquarius | Sagittarius | Pisces | Cancer |
| Pisces | Pisces | Sagittarius | Aquarius | Libra |

# Compatibility At Work and Business

| YOUR SIGN | GREAT | GOOD | FAIR | NOPE |
|---|---|---|---|---|
| Aries | Aquarius | Sagittarius | Virgo | Capricorn |
| Taurus | Libra | Taurus | Pisces | Gemini |
| Gemini | Aries | Leo | Libra | Pisces |
| Cancer | Taurus | Capricorn | Virgo | Scorpio |
| Leo | Scorpio | Virgo | Aquarius | Sagittarius |
| Virgo | Gemini | Leo | Cancer | Aquarius |
| Libra | Taurus | Gemini | Aries | Capricorn |
| Scorpio | Virgo | Capricorn | Aquarius | Taurus |
| Sagittarius | Pisces | Aries | Leo | Cancer |
| Capricorn | Scorpio | Cancer | Taurus | Leo |
| Aquarius | Aries | Leo | Sagittarius | Pisces |
| Pisces | Virgo | Sagittarius | Leo | Scorpio |

# Best Times, Lucky Times for Your Sign

**14**

The chapters on the sun signs each contained a list of correspondences that included best and worst days for your sign. This section will go into more detail about how the days and hours will affect you. Each day of the week is each ruled by one of the seven planets that are visible with the naked eye (Neptune and Pluto are discluded). Check out your sign's ruling planet, your sign, and its day to spot those that are likely to be lucky for you.

## Planetary Rulership by Day

| Planet | Sign | Day |
| --- | --- | --- |
| Mars | Aries | Tuesday |
| Venus | Taurus | Friday |
| Mercury | Gemini | Wednesday |
| Moon | Cancer | Monday |
| Sun | Leo | Sunday |
| Mercury | Virgo | Wednesday |
| Venus | Libra | Friday |
| Mars | Scorpio | Tuesday |
| Jupiter | Sagittarius | Thursday |
| Saturn | Capricorn | Saturday |
| Saturn | Aquarius | Saturday |
| Jupiter | Pisces | Thursday |

## Planetary Rulership by Hour

This is more complex, because the following table shows the days of the week along the top and every hour of the day in the left hand column. Track down and across to check which planet rules the particular hour on any day of the week. The information

| Hour | Sun | Mon | Tue | Wed | Thu | Fri | Sat |
|------|-----|-----|-----|-----|-----|-----|-----|
| **A.M.** | | | | | | | |
| 1 | Sun | Moon | Mars | Mercury | Jupiter | Venus | Saturn |
| 2 | Venus | Saturn | Sun | Moon | Mars | Mercury | Jupiter |
| 3 | Mercury | Jupiter | Venus | Saturn | Sun | Moon | Mars |
| 4 | Moon | Mars | Mercury | Jupiter | Venus | Saturn | Sun |
| 5 | Saturn | Sun | Moon | Mars | Mercury | Jupiter | Venus |
| 6 | Jupiter | Venus | Saturn | Sun | Moon | Mars | Mercury |
| 7 | Mars | Mercury | Jupiter | Venus | Saturn | Sun | Moon |
| 8 | Sun | Moon | Mars | Mercury | Jupiter | Venus | Saturn |
| 9 | Venus | Saturn | Sun | Moon | Mars | Mercury | Jupiter |
| 10 | Mercury | Jupiter | Venus | Saturn | Sun | Moon | Mars |
| 11 | Moon | Mars | Mercury | Jupiter | Venus | Saturn | Sun |
| 12 | Saturn | Sun | Moon | Mars | Mercury | Jupiter | Venus |
| **P.M.** | | | | | | | |
| 13 | Jupiter | Venus | Saturn | Sun | Moon | Mars | Mercury |
| 14 | Mars | Mercury | Jupiter | Venus | Saturn | Sun | Moon |
| 15 | Sun | Moon | Mars | Mercury | Jupiter | Venus | Saturn |
| 16 | Venus | Saturn | Sun | Moon | Mars | Mercury | Jupiter |
| 17 | Mercury | Jupiter | Venus | Saturn | Sun | Moon | Mars |
| 18 | Moon | Mars | Mercury | Jupiter | Venus | Saturn | Sun |
| 19 | Saturn | Sun | Moon | Mars | Mercury | Jupiter | Venus |
| 20 | Jupiter | Venus | Saturn | Sun | Moon | Mars | Mercury |
| 21 | Mars | Mercury | Jupiter | Venus | Saturn | Sun | Moon |
| 22 | Sun | Moon | Mars | Mercury | Jupiter | Venus | Saturn |
| 23 | Venus | Saturn | Sun | Moon | Mars | Mercury | Jupiter |
| 24 | Mercury | Jupiter | Venus | Saturn | Sun | Moon | Mars |

**Note:** In countries where British Summer Time or Daylight Saving is in operation during part of the year, deduct one hour during the affected summer months.

that follows will show you how the energies of each planet affect each hour. The Rulership by Day table above has already shown you which planet rules your sign, so you can now choose an hour that links with your planet to make a start on a particularly important matter. This kind of astrology is called *electional* astrology, because this way you get to *elect* the right time on the right day for a special event.

## A Sun Hour

*A joyful and successful hour*

A Sun hour should be a happy and joyful one. Anything that you are considering setting out to do should have a great outcome if you start doing it during a Sun hour. A celebration that begins now should turn out to be a great success. If you are arranging a day or an evening in the company of someone you love, you will have a great time. This is a good hour in which to set off for a holiday or to treat yourself to something that you fancy. It is even a great time to make love.

Anything to do with children or young people will go well if started at this time, and even if you only spend time kicking a ball around with your children, you will thoroughly enjoy yourself. This is a great hour for success in business or in a social setting, and if you need to be the center of attention for some reason, there couldn't be a better time. The Sun's association with gold and jewelry makes this a terrific hour in which to buy a ring or any other sparkly token of love for yourself or for your partner. Business matters should be also successful during this phase. Remember that the Sun god, Apollo, loved music. Therefore, if you want to play music, go to a musical event, or even to put on your favorite CD and relax for a while, this is a wonderful time for it. If you can do something that looks like being fun—even a game of Monopoly with the children—do it now.

## A Moon Hour

*An hour of sensitive feelings*

There is good news and bad news connected to the Moon hour because this can be one of those times when your emotions will burst through whatever has been keeping them in check. There are occasions when you can put up with almost anything, but this is not one of them. Things that usually pass you by almost unnoticed will get you down now. If there happens to be a Full Moon or an eclipse occurring on this day, you will suffer from a form of premenstrual tension—and this will be the case even if you are too old for it or if you are a man!

On the other hand, this is a great hour for home and family concerns. Anything from a family gathering to talking around the dining table with your loved ones or simply relaxing in front of the television with your nearest and dearest will be great now. House moves, decorating or refurbishing or anything else of that nature will go well if it is started during a Moon hour. If you want to contact older family members or spend time with them, there couldn't be a better hour. You may feel restless during this time, so try to arrange a trip out somewhere rather than getting down to work or doing chores.

Sometimes the Moon acts as a trigger to events, so if you are waiting for something to happen, it should do so now. The influence of the Moon could make you quite perceptive and even psychic for a while.

## A Mars Hour

*An active hour*

Mars is the action planet, so if there is something you need to do that requires action and activity, this is the time to go for it. There are a whole host of possible scenarios here but some ideas might include doing a tough, dirty or heavy job either at work or in the home or perhaps working on the car. If you need to make a mental or physical effort at work for any purpose, get started on this during a Mars hour.

If you need to state your case or to put your foot down this could be the time to do so, but remember that Mars was the Roman god of war, so stand up for yourself by all means but don't take things to the point where you start a real feud. Dealings with men will go well, and this applies to business matters or calling a builder or a workman to do something in your house. Passion in all its forms comes to the fore now, so lovemaking or passionate feelings will be reciprocated. If you are passionate about sports, you will be more energetic and competitive than usual and you could end up the winner in any game in which you participate during this hour.

Even if you have a passion for something as innocuous as stamp collecting, you will find what you want and get where you want to be if you make the effort now. On a less pleasant note, you could find yourself at the dentist or undergoing some other kind of minor surgical procedure.

# A Mercury Hour

*A busy time with much contact with others*

Mercury was the messenger of the Roman gods and he often had to do the dirty work for Jupiter and Apollo. You can expect to make a few phone calls and deal with correspondence during this hour, but this doesn't mean that you will be expected to have to do someone's dirty work. It is simply a case of having to make contact with people and to communicate. You won't get much peace and quiet now, but you will manage to get a lot done.

There may be contact with brothers, sisters and neighbors at this time, and if you need help or cooperation from such people, this is a good time to ask for it. Mercury rules short journeys, so trips to the shops or errands of any kind will go well now. If you need to get a vehicle fixed, this is a good time to arrange it.

Activities with young people and even indulging in gentle sport or other amusing activity will be good for you. You may be a bit rushed for a while, but you shouldn't be unhappy.

# A Jupiter Hour

*A time to expand your horizons*

Jupiter was the king of the ancient gods and he could bring good or bad luck depending upon his mood. As far as an hourly reading is concerned, there are a whole host of things that are worth doing during this period. Jupiter rules expansion of horizons so you could book a trip or even arrange to travel at this time, and this is especially applicable to long-distance trips. Business that involves overseas customers or even dealing with foreigners in your own land will be successful during this hour. If you have any legal or official matters to cope with, this is a good time for them. Jupiter rules education, so it's a good time to open your books and get down to studying, if this is applicable. Even if you only need to study how some new household appliance or computer program works, this is a good time to get your head around it. Jupiter rules belief and by extension religion, philosophy and spirituality, so if you intend to go to a church meeting, a spiritualist event, a psychic event or even to sit and think about what moves you, this is the hour for it.

Some see Jupiter as a lucky planet and it is true that it is associated with gambling, especially horseracing. Therefore, if you intend to put a little wager on a horse or try your luck with the lottery, this is as good an hour as any for it. If the lottery is drawn during one of your Jupiter hours, this is even more likely to bring you luck.

Sometimes Jupiter will bring a breakthrough in business, but it can also bring setbacks. These, however, are usually followed by an improvement in circumstances or changes that need to be made.

## A Venus Hour

*A time for love, pleasure and self-indulgence*

Venus is the Roman goddess of love, so it is easy to see what this hour is all about! If you are planning a romantic meeting with a lover or even with a potential mate, this is the time for it. Romantic evenings indoors are equally well starred. Obviously, this becomes a good hour in which to get engaged or married, but it is an equally good time in which to start a business or some other moneymaking enterprise. If you want to buy something special for the home, try to do it during this hour, and if what you are considering buying is good to look at, so much the better. Practical jobs of a creative nature will go well during this hour, so if you are into gardening, cooking or making attractive objects of any kind, this is the time in which to do it. Farming, working the land or even buying stock for a farm should all go well if started at this hour. Money can be made from projects that are started now, especially if there is someone else who is involved—although it would be wise to check out the data for the other person as well as your own.

## A Saturn Hour

*A time for work and for sorting out details*

Saturn can be a hard taskmaster, so this is the best hour for getting difficult jobs done and dusted. If you need to talk to a boss or to someone in a position of authority, try to schedule this for a Saturn hour.

Parents and other older people are more likely to be helpful to you at this time, although you will have to put yourself out or make an effort to contact them. This is a good hour in which to start a long-term project, to put down roots or to try to achieve stability in any sphere of your life.

# Try another practical guide in the
# ORION PLAIN AND SIMPLE series